In the
Presence
of
Grace

In the
Presence
of
Grace

Prayers & Meditations
to Grow By

LAUREN E. MYERS

Advancing the Ministries of the Gospel
AMG *Publishers*

God's Word to you is our highest calling.

In the Presence of Grace
Copyright © 2004 by Lauren Erika Myers
Published by AMG Publishers
6815 Shallowford Rd.
Chattanooga, TN 37421

Unless otherwise indicated, all Scripture quotations are taken from the HOLY BIBLE:
NEW INTERNATIONAL VERSION® NIV®. Copyright © 1973, 1978, 1984 by
International Bible Society. Used by permission of Zondervan Publishing House.
All rights reserved.

Scripture quotations marked (KJV) are taken from The Holy Bible, *King James Version*

Scripture quotations marked (CEV) Bible are taken from the Contemporary English
Version. Copyright © 1995 by the American Bible Society. All rights reserved.

ISBN 0-89957-137-9

First printing—July 2004

Cover designed by Meyers Design, Shepherd, Texas
Interior design and typesetting by Pro Production, Nanuet, New York
Edited and Proofread by Bob Land of Land on Demand, Dan Penwell,
    Tricia Lawrence, Warren Baker, and Rick Steele

Printed in the United States of America
09 08 07 06 05 04 –B– 8 7 6 5 4 3 2 1

I dedicate this book to JEM, my husband; and to my grandmother, Thirza Asenath "Miss T" Williams, whose godly example led me to Christ as a little child; to her niece Miriam Rose "Aunt Rose" Elliott, the matriarch whose legendary early morning prayer vigils continue to give us strength; to my best friend—my mother; and to Lynn, whose candor, and unfailing good humor helps me keep things in perspective.

Foreword

It is with great joy that I commend to you this devotional guide written by Lauren Myers. The many hours of prayerful and thoughtful reflection are evidenced by the content of each daily scriptural reading, the insightful comments, and the subsequent prayer.

Indeed, the devotions convey principles applicable to all no matter the geographic location. All who read the devotional presentations will be inspired, encouraged, and challenged to trust the Lord and to be thankful in all and for all things (1 Thess. 5:18, Eph. 5:20). To be sure these pages are filled with insights that have come from the heart of a committed pastor's wife of many years.

It is my privilege to know Lauren and her husband, Pastor J. Edsil Myers. To know them is to know that the words penned in these pages have not only been expressed in writing but also experienced in the various churches they have faithfully served.

May the Lord illuminate your heart as you meditate on the thoughts contained in this devotional guide.

—Edwin Cordero, D. Min.
Pastor/Presbyter, Assemblies of God

Acknowledgments

First, I give honor and grateful praise to God for his gift. Heartfelt thanks to the friends who never doubted the value of this project and encouraged and prayed me through to its completion. I shall be forever indebted to my editors who know the rules and see to it that I follow them; to my god-send, writing mentor Elaine Wright Colvin; to Dr. Edwin Cordero whose enthusiasm for the project gave me strength; to Dr. Calvin Miller who convinced me that all I needed was to be me; to Peggy, Jeff, and Mark—my personal cheering section; to Lynn who tells me when *it doesn't flow* and makes me rewrite; to the directors and the many gifted and compassionate faculty members of the Florida Christian Writers' Conference; and to Kristy Dykes for direction, friendship, and encouragement.

With immeasurable gratitude to my brother, Paul, for his unshakeable faith in me, to Mom, my best friend; to my wonderful children Newton, Simon, and Lauren—you will always be my highest achievement. Thanks for your support, your love, and your friendship.

Lastly, to my husband who understood my compulsion to write at odd hours and bought me my first lighted pen. Your saying, "Mommy, you can do it," makes all the difference in the world. I love you.

You may have wondered why, after Adam and Eve sinned, God did not just abandon the whole idea of fellowship with man. Surely it would have been easier to simply remove the two people involved and start all over again rather than have an entire universe caught in sin's aftermath. Could it be that the soul is so infinitely precious that the destruction of even one would leave an echoing void through eons of eternity? Whatever the reason, God chose redemption over annihilation.

The Bible says, "But when the time had fully come, God sent his Son, born of a woman born under the law, to redeem those under the law" (Gal. 4:4). Joseph, his father, was told to name the baby "Jesus, because he [would] save his people from their sins" (Matt. 1:21).

So what does that mean for us today? No matter how far we have strayed—no matter the choices we, like Eve, have allowed our curiosity to lead us into—God still desires to save us. He takes no pleasure in our suffering or in our death and ultimate separation from his presence. In spite of all our weaknesses, we are precious to God. We are the crowning jewels of creation, and he gave all he had for our salvation.

Day 1

PROMISE OF REDEMPTION

"Have you eaten from the tree that I commanded you not to eat from?"
—Genesis 3:11

PRAYER:
Dear Jesus, thank you for your great and unfathomable love; thank you for my salvation. Amen.

Day 2

"My ears had heard of you but now my eyes have seen you."
—Job 2:5

A strong Christian heritage may be evident in the memories we treasure. We may fondly remember old songs and Bible games. The smell of crayons and glue may take us back to our childhood and vacation Bible school. Our parents or grandparents may have been the men and women of God whose imprint of grace remains indelible upon our lives.

Regardless of the memories we have, unless we make a personal commitment to Christ and accept his forgiveness for our sins, we are in no better shape than those who have no knowledge of Christ at all. We learn many things about God during the course of a lifetime, but salvation can neither be taught nor inherited. Let us make sure what we know of Christ is not what we have learned by living around Christians or by going to church.

A personal relationship with Jesus involves more than academic awareness. Rather, it speaks of an inner change and heart-involved commitment to furthering God's kingdom on earth. Do you just know about him, or are you secure in the reality that he is the Lord and Savior of your life?

PRAYER:
*Dear Jesus,
I invite you into
my life today.
Please forgive my
sins and help me to
truly know you.
Amen.*

In the Scripture text, we are left with the impression that sin is a basic and permanent part of human nature. The same idea is repeated in Jeremiah 17:9: "The heart is deceitful above all things and beyond cure." In the New Testament, Paul gives a plaintive lament. "For what I do is not the good I want to do; no, the evil I do not want to do—this I keep on doing. . . .What a wretched man I am!" (Rom. 7:19, 24). We are not naturally good, though we are all born innocent—without the consciousness of right and wrong. Christ tells us, "For all have sinned and fall short of the glory of God" (Rom. 3:23).

Is there hope? Can we become good? Through the blood of Jesus, we can. He, who is incapable of sinning, accepted the punishment for our sins and gave us his righteousness in return. When God the Father sees us, he does not see our own pitiful attempts at holiness. Instead, he sees righteousness credited to our account. We are good, holy, and pure—only in Jesus Christ.

*Mrs. Cecil F. Alexander, 1848.

Day 3

JUST HOW GOOD ARE WE?

"Never again will I curse the ground because of man, even though every inclination of his heart is evil from childhood."
—Genesis 8:21

PRAYER:
Dear Father, thank you for sending Jesus to be righteousness for us. Help me to remember: He died that we might be forgiven/he died to make us good/That we might go at last to Heaven/Saved by His precious blood.* Amen.

Day 4

Do You Have the Birthmark?

"The blood will be a sign for you on the houses where you are; and when I see the blood, I will pass over you."
—Genesis 12:13

Prayer:
Dear Jesus, thank you for the sacrifice of your blood for my sins. Help me to wear the mark of the new birth proudly and to point others to your cross. Amen.

Science tells us that a birthmark is an area of discolored skin present from birth caused by malformations of pigment cells. While "strawberries" and freckles are the most common, birthmarks can take the shape and size of almost anything.*

Christians bear a mark as indelible and distinctive as any birthmark. It is at once intensely personal and completely universal. This mark is called "The Blood." As the death angel passed through the land of Egypt exacting vengeance for Pharaoh's defiance of Israel's God, the blood became instrumental in preserving life. All through history, the sacrificial blood of animals served as a palliative measure to cover sins so man could have limited fellowship with God. There was no cure for sin—none, that is, until Jesus came. Scripture says, "For you know that it was not with perishable things such as silver or gold that you were redeemed from the empty way of life handed down to you from your forefathers, but with the precious blood of Christ, a lamb without blemish or defect" (1 Pet. 1:18, 19).

When we ask Christ into our lives, we are born into the family of God by the same blood that was spilled on Calvary. True, like most birthmarks, the blood is singularly unpopular. Some have even tried to remove it from hymnals and church sermons and so present a less objectionable method of salvation. The mark, however, will always remain because "without the shedding of blood there is no forgiveness" (Heb. 9:22). Are your sins forgiven? Do you have the birthmark? Then wear it well.

*The American Medical Association Home Medical Encyclopedia (New York: Random House, 1989).

A holy desperation characterizes the true child of God. Nothing assuages this thirst of the soul but God. Once his presence is realized, nothing satisfies but more and more of him. The Beatitudes tell us that if we hunger and thirst after righteousness, we will be filled (Matt. 5:6). Yes, we will be filled with the Spirit of God. His life will be expressed through us——filled but never satisfied.

To be complacent about our walk with God is to admit we have not really been in his presence. Although we experience great joy from our times of communion and fellowship with the Father, we are sharply reminded of our sinfulness every time we encounter him. His holiness shines in such blinding contrast to our own lives that we can only cry in despair, like Isaiah, "Woe is me, for I am undone; because I am a man of unclean lips" (Isa. 6:5 KJV).

David paints a graphic picture as he compares his desire for God to being in the desert and suffering the pangs of thirst with no water in sight. One need not wonder what would be the foremost thought in the mind of someone who is dying from lack of water. The overwhelming physical need would doubtless obliterate every other concern.

Are we desperate for the indwelling presence of God in our lives? Does our need to be like him take precedence over the world's opinion and philosophies? If we hunger after God, he will fill us. If we search for his presence, we will find him when we search with all our hearts (Jer. 29:13). ❧

Day 5

An Earnest Desire

"O God, you are my God, earnestly I seek you; my soul thirsts for you, my body longs for you, in a dry and weary land where there is no water."
—Psalm 63:1

PRAYER:
*Dear Father,
I seek your presence
in my life. Fill me to
overflowing with
your Holy Spirit.
Amen.*

Day 6

*"He is like a
tree planted by
streams of water."*
—Psalm 1:3

How does one go from being a sinner to the tree described in this passage? First, the Father draws or woos us to acknowledge Jesus as Lord. Next, the seed of the Word is sown in our hearts through preaching, when someone tells us about Christ or something we read emphasizes our need for a savior. Whatever method is employed, the "hearing" of the Word occurs, and faith is activated.

Once the seed is sown, the Holy Spirit brings about germination. Words cease to be just words and become truths that God speaks directly to us. This transformation, in turn, makes us alive in Christ with the potential to grow in our understanding of him as we engage our hearts and minds to study his Word, the Bible.

As we cultivate fellowship with the Father through prayer and worshiping with other believers, we begin to take on new growth and new life. Eventually, like the tree in our meditation, we blossom and bear fruit. Love, joy, peace, patience, kindness, gentleness, and self-control will be evident to those around us.

PRAYER:
*Lord Jesus,
I just want to grow
and become more like
you as I immerse
myself in the study
of your Word.
Amen.*

What does it mean to walk with God? Is it even possible? We may conjure up images of Jesus and the disciples walking the dusty roads of Nazareth and Galilee, but that is hardly possible for us to do today. Let us suppose this statement recorded of Enoch is within the bound of possibility. Can we do the same?

First of all, a walk with God does not necessarily mean a visible person matching steps along a path. It has little to do with whether or not we consciously feel a "presence" at all times, and has everything to do with what we accept by faith. If I believe in an all-powerful, ever-present God, then I should also be aware that wherever I go and whatever I do, his presence goes with me. There should be no need to stop what I'm doing or to hide if God suddenly made himself visible to my natural eyes.

I walk with him by involving him in every aspect of my life and in seeking to glorify and honor his name. Our walk with God is reflected when we ask questions like "Am I doing as Jesus would?" when faced with tough decisions. We walk with God when we pray, "Let your will be done," and are submissive to what God does, even if we do not immediately agree.

So, can we be like Enoch? I think we can. 🌿

Day 7

WALKING WITH GOD

Enoch walked with God; then he was no more, because God took him away.
—Genesis 5:24

PRAYER:
*Dear Lord Jesus,
I affirm my faith in
your presence with me
every day of my life.
I choose to walk in
step with your will.
Amen.*

Day 8

"Know therefore that the LORD your God is God; he is the faithful God, keeping His covenant of love to a thousand generations of those who love him and keep his commands."
—Deuteronomy 7:9

PRAYER:
Great and awesome God, there is no one as faithful as you are. Father, you remain the same through all the ages of eternity, and I believe your promise that you will always be the same. Help me to be faithful in my love and service to you. Amen.

A covenant denotes a binding and solemn agreement made between two or more persons. The same word is used to describe the promises of God to humanity recorded for us in the Bible. Why would he covenant with us, knowing full well we would never live up to our side of the bargain? Indeed, we cannot keep our part of the agreement, because unconditional commitment is not a part of our nature. God, because of his great love, bound himself to us in an irrevocable pledge. The terms of the agreement are inviolate "for his name's sake."

What does this mean for us? The name of God is synonymous with his nature—that is, his inability to lie, dissemble, break a promise, be unfaithful, be unjust, or be partial. In short, God is completely unable to display any of the vices that abound in us. No wonder the writer says, "If we are faithless, he will remain faithful, for he cannot disown himself" (2 Tim. 2:13). God will never develop a tolerance for sin, but he will always love the sinner. His love endures forever. 🌿

Are you wondering if God will be on time to rescue you from your present dilemma? Are you feeling somehow he may let you down or that there will never be an answer to your prayer? Be encouraged. God is still who he says he is. He has promised:

Strength—Equal to your daily need for as long as you live (Deut. 33:25).

Refuge—The eternal God is your refuge, and underneath are the everlasting arms (Deut. 33:27).

Unfailing Love—Though the mountains be shaken and the hills be removed, yet my unfailing love for you will not be shaken (Isa. 54:10).

Divine Insight—Call to me and I will answer you and tell you great and unsearchable things that you do not know (Jer. 33:3).

Answers to Prayer—If you abide in me and my words abide in you, you shall ask what you will and it shall be given you (John 15:7).

If you are anxious or saddened by some turn of events in your life, grab hold of a promise. God will come through for you. ❧

Day 9

As Good as His Word

"God is not a man, that he should lie, nor a son of man, that he should change his mind."
—Numbers 23:19

PRAYER:
Lord, I so often judge you by my own inconsistencies. Please forgive my unbelief and help me to trust you unconditionally. Amen.

Day 10

"The people remained at a distance, while Moses approached the thick darkness where God was."

—Exodus 20:21

We most frequently associate God with light and rightly so, as he describes himself as both the Father of lights and the light of the world. We should not, however, assume that if darkness surrounds us, the presence of God has somehow left us.

At the giving of the law on Sinai, God made his appearance in flames of fire, and the people were terrified. He changed the plan a bit and clothed himself in thick darkness instead. Cringing in fear, the people removed themselves to what they considered a safe distance and begged Moses to speak to God on their behalf. Moses chose to press in and linger in the presence of God. He stayed so long his face began to glow. It was such an awesome sight to the children of Israel they asked him to cover his face (Exod. 34:33).

All this came about because Moses was willing to go into the thick darkness where God was. Physical things, like darkness or light, cannot hinder God. In our worst circumstance, if we look long enough, we will find him. Jonah, in complete darkness in the belly of the great fish at the bottom of the ocean, cried to the Lord, and God heard him. Do not run from the darkness. Rather, run to the One to whom the darkness and the light both shine as clearest day.

PRAYER:
Father, help me to remember you are everywhere, and to find you even in the seemingly dark circumstances of life. Amen.

Sometimes we struggle in our prayer time to establish connection with God. We send up a barrage of petitions only to feel like the words are hitting the ceiling, going no farther. We are assured in the Word of God that he answers every prayer prayed according to the will of the Father. It is equally clear that God inhabits or lives in our praise. In other words, praise draws him closer than any other activity we can perform.

Why should we praise God? If one takes a quick trip through the book of Psalms, reasons like his goodness, his greatness, his great love, and his kindness immediately spring to the forefront. To those attributes we could add his awesome deeds, the majesty of his name, as well as signs and wonders. The list is literally endless.

We do not have to keep a diary of noteworthy events in our own lives in order to praise God. The little things—sunshine, air, and the breath we take for granted every day—all provide reason enough. Our moods should not detract from our ability to offer worship to God. He remains who he is in spite of the changes we go through.

The Bible echoes with great victories that came when people overlooked their predicaments and simply offered praise. Joshua, Jehoshaphat, Paul, and Silas, to name a few, all had miraculous deliverances, born of heartfelt praise. We can determine to practice praise. It may be that God will fill our bodily temples with his glory just as he did the tabernacle of old.

Day 11

THE POWER
OF PRAISE

"The trumpeters and singers joined in unison, as with one voice, to give praise and thanks to the LORD *. . . Then the temple of the* LORD *was filled with a cloud for the glory of the* LORD *filled the temple of God."*
—2 Chronicles 5:13, 14

PRAYER:
Dear Heavenly Father, so often I come before you with a wish list and forget to thank you for the blessings of the previous day. I praise you now for all the blessings of my life, and most of all for who you are. Amen.

Day 12

HOW GREAT
THOU ART

*"When I consider
your heavens, the
work of your fingers,
what is man?"*
—Psalm 8:3, 4

PRAYER:
*My Father,
I stand in amazement
at your greatness.
Thanks for choosing
humanity to be
the centerpiece
of creation.
Amen.*

A s the evening shadows lengthened, blending and reducing the vibrant colors of the day into softer and gentler hues, a giant canvas unfolded in the western sky. One could easily descry clumps of brush, tall slender trees, and emerald pools of water throughout the landscape. Numerous animals in arrested motion dotted the limitless plain.

Moment by moment the scene changed, adding a depth and clarity to the picture that made the use of a camera an act of futility. Brush-stroke by invisible brush-stroke, the Maestro covered the sky with awesome beauty, right up to the moment when the sun slipped in dusky fire beneath the horizon. We gazed at the sky until the first star appeared, too awed to do anything but marvel at the handiwork of our Creator.

Standing in the gathering darkness, still breathless from the glory of the evening, I struggled to understand why a God of such greatness takes time to fellowship with us and to desire our love. Perhaps, if we were angelic beings completely pure and holy, even as he is, then maybe it would be easier to comprehend why he allows us to call him Father.

Failing to grasp the richness of the Father's grace, my heart lifted in simple gratitude to be his child and to be a witness to the beauty of the world he created.

The single most amazing thing about contemplating the greatness of God is that one can draw no parallels. Consequently, in a short time both word and thought are exhausted and we fall back on faith in all he says he is and all he has shown himself to be.

Through the ages God has been described as:

The Great I Am
The Righteous Judge
A God of compassion and mercy
The Lion of the Tribe of Judah
The Rose of Sharon
The Creator
The Man of Sorrows
Emmanuel
The One Who Was, and Is, and
    Is to Come
The Savior of the World
The Friend of Sinners

No wonder God asks, "To whom will you compare me or count me equal? To whom will you liken me that we may be compared?" (Isa. 46:5). May we, like the psalmist, joyfully proclaim, "O Lord, our Lord, how majestic is your name in all the earth!" (Psalm 8:1, 9). Today as you contemplate the majesty of God, remember this awesome God loves you and wants to be your friend.

Day 13

WHO IS LIKE HIM?

*"Who among the gods
is like you,
O LORD?
Who is like you—
majestic in holiness,
awesome in glory,
working wonders?"*
—Exodus 15:11

PRAYER:
*Awesome God,
my Father and friend,
thank you for making
yourself available to
all who come to you.
Thank you for being
my savior.
Amen.*

Day 14

COUNT YOUR BLESSINGS

"But be sure to fear the LORD and serve him faithfully with all your heart; consider what great things he has done for you."
—1 Samuel 12:24

PRAYER:
Father, I know I sometimes forget to thank you for your blessings in my life, and I overlook the small things. Today I just want to tell you I am grateful, not only for what I see, but for the knowledge that you work everything for my eternal good. Amen.

In times of great difficulty, we often feel alone and forgotten. As troubles multiply, we may even begin to believe nothing will ever be quite the same again. In a sense, we forget the goodness of the Lord.

How does one regain a realistic perspective? We can start by thanking God for being alive as each day presents new opportunities for us to lead someone to him. We can certainly give thanks for salvation, the hope of everlasting life and immediate access to the Father, the protection of angels, and the indwelling presence of the Holy Spirit. Then there is our family and other special people God has placed in our lives. As we list our past blessings, we reaffirm God's continuing faithfulness. Only you know what he has done for you over the years. Think a moment and begin to give thanks. Remember to include the little things as well as the obvious, outstanding blessings.

If you have been doing this little exercise, by now the river Gratitude should be overflowing its banks. Confidence in God should be rising like incense to his throne. We have an Almighty God who cares for us and loves each of us as if there were no one else in the world. Oh, things may not always be easy or go well from our standpoint, but all things, every little, itty-bitty thing, is working together for our eternal good. So,

> "Count your blessings . . . Name them one by one
> And it will surprise you . . . What the Lord hath done."*

"Count Your Blessings" by Johnson Oatman Jr. (1856–1922) and Edwin O. Excel (1851–1921).

What kind of a general would send a choir to fight a war? If a huge army threatened your city and began setting parameters to lay siege, would you be comfortable seeing the mass choir going out to confront them? Wouldn't you wonder why your own armed forces weren't trying to attack the enemy before it got organized?

God, however, has a reputation for doing things differently. He told the king to use a weapon few had ever used before—the weapon called praise. When the enemy stands in battle formation against us, or we are being bombarded by sickness or financial reverses, the last thing we want to do is call the choir or even to sing ourselves. But the Bible tells us the joy of the Lord not only gives strength, it *is* our strength. Maybe, when things are at their worst and our spirits are at their lowest, a song of praise can be the means of our deliverance.

What are we saying when we praise God in adversity? We are proclaiming our faith and our confidence in him. We are positively stating no matter what we see around us, we recognize God's sovereign authority and power to completely deliver us. Have you exhausted all other weapons without seeing victory? Try the power of praise.

Day 15

A MOST UNUSUAL WEAPON

Jehoshaphat appointed men to sing to the LORD and to praise him [and] the LORD set ambushes.
—2 Chronicles 20: 21, 22

PRAYER:
Dear Father, I praise you for your grace, your mercy, and your power to deliver. Thank you for victory over every weapon the devil brings against me. Amen.

Day 16

PRAISING
AT ALL TIMES

*"I will extol the
LORD at all times;
his praise will always
be on my lips."*
—Psalm 34:1

God's absolute constancy and his total reliability in all situations set him far above human thought and action. We change with every circumstance. When things are going well, we are quick to praise God and to rejoice in our mountaintop experience. When the scene changes, however, and trials, stress, and exhaustion enter the picture, frustration sets in and we sometime lose our song. Praises become ho-hum as our focus turns inward instead of above to the one who controls the motions of our lives.

Surely, when the psalmist declared he would praise God at all times, he must have known there would be days clouded by perplexity and sorrow. Who, like David, could better explain all the situations that could vex our spirit and sap emotional strength? Still, he resolved to extol—praise or bless—the Lord at all times.

When we understand we do not praise God simply for what he does but because of who he is, we will also know offering up praises and thanksgiving is the very least we can do.

PRAYER:
*O Lord, my God,
how excellent you
are! I look beyond
even the good in my
life today and give
you praise just
because you are God.
Amen.*

The beach lay panting beneath the orange glow of sunset, white sands still sizzling from the day's onslaught of the Caribbean sun. I watched as the waves barreled in and shattered in white foam against the rocks. For a time, it seemed as if the sea redoubled its efforts to claim another foot of beach with each succeeding wave, only to fall within the same boundaries as before. In spite of its immeasurable might and limitless depths, the ocean could only remain subject to the authority of God.

Our mighty ocean may be beyond our power to change or control. Still, we can rest assured we will not be overwhelmed. Don't be fooled by the roar of the waves; everything in the universe bows to the will of God. Deep waters will neither drown us nor sweep us away (Isa. 43:2). God sets the boundaries, and nothing crosses over unless he wills it. ❧

Day 17

DIVINE BOUNDARIES

"You set a boundary they cannot cross; never again will they cover the earth."
—Psalm 104:9

PRAYER:
*Almighty God,
I am secure because
you are in control.
I rest in your
protective care.
Amen.*

Day 18

"Give thanks in all circumstances, for this is God's will for you in Christ Jesus."

—1 Thessalonians 5:18

Every home health nurse in the agency knew Ma Brown. One of the first patients to be registered when the agency started twenty years earlier, Ma Brown also knew just about everyone. When a "new" nurse visited her, it became standard procedure for Ma Brown to sit her down and find out "who her people was" before anything else was done. She would often stop in the middle of a sentence to ask if the nurse had children of her own. "Sho' nuff?" she would reply if the nurse said yes. "You look like a little girl yourself."

Ma Brown never fussed about being completely blind in her left eye or seemed overly concerned her right eye was failing fast. She never wasted time talking about her diabetes or her legs that were sometimes so swollen and painful she could not get up from her recliner without help. Ma Brown praised God for the woman who took her to the doctor and the one who took her to church every now and then. Ma Brown even praised God for her "good-for-nothing nephew who hardly home no-how." She would get so excited talking about Jesus. She would rock back and forth and tap her cane on the floor for emphasis. "Yes Lawd, he sho' nuff good to me."

Many knew her as the brash old lady who complained if you finished the visit in half an hour and did not stop to talk for a little while. Others may remember her as the woman who gave step-by-step directions on how to do her bath. Still others cherish the example of a dear saint who practiced in everything to give thanks.

(continued next page)

It is so easy to be grateful and happy when everything goes according to plan. Giving thanks becomes harder when our health, security, or well-being is threatened. We are not expected to be thankful for all the bad things that happen. Rather, we should praise God in the midst of it all. Praises flow easier when we remember God loves us and promises to be with us no matter what we go through. ❦

Day 18

PRAYER:
Father, how grateful
I am for your
presence each moment
of my life. You have
never failed to be
there through my
illnesses and my
times of loneliness,
and in the middle
of my despair.
Thank you for being
so good to me.
Amen.

Day 19

NAME ONE THING
GOD CAN'T DO

*"For nothing is
impossible with God."*
—Luke 1:37

The sum of our peace of mind is the difference between what we know with our heads and what we believe in our hearts. Most of us would answer almost impatiently if asked to name something God cannot do. On the other hand, if we are asked, "Do you worry and fret when faced with difficulties?" Most of us would answer, "Yes."

Mary found herself in a peculiar situation. She was a virgin engaged to Joseph and had just been told by an angel she was about to have a child. Then, as now, the idea of being pregnant by the power of the Holy Spirit would not be well received. She faced ridicule from the villagers, ostracism by her family, and almost certain dissolution of the marriage agreement between her and Joseph. She voiced her misgivings, and the angel reminded her that with God all things are possible. That was all Mary needed to hear. Her answer eloquently speaks of her faith and trust in God: "I am the Lord's servant. May it be to me as you have said" (Luke 1:38). Rest became possible when head knowledge became the conviction of her heart. She believed with her whole being that God could do all things.

Are you faced with an impossible situation? Believe with your heart what your mind knows to be true: Nothing is impossible with God. ❧

PRAYER:
*My Father, I am
frequently dwarfed by
problems that seem to
have no solution.
Please help me to
remember you have
the answers I need,
for nothing is
impossible for you.
Amen.*

Our perception of who we are and the ability we possess will always influence what we accomplish. The scouts Moses sent to spy out the land of Canaan returned with good news and bad news. The good news was that the land was fertile and just what they hoped for. The bad news was worse than they imagined: There were giants guarding the land. Not only that, the scouts said in the giants' eyes, the men of Israel looked like grasshoppers.

All the scouts who shared this pessimistic view died without ever entering Canaan. Caleb and Joshua saw themselves as men through whom God could work to overcome obstacles. They declared confidence in God, and he honored their faith.

Is the enemy casting a massive shadow over what is promised to you? Look your giant in the eye and tell him you will take possession of what is yours. God says you can do it. If you step out by faith, you will succeed. 🌾

Day 20

I THINK I CAN, I SAID I COULD

"We should go up and take possession of the land, for we can certainly do it."
—Numbers 13:30

PRAYER:
Lord Jesus, you have not given me a spirit of fear but of power, of love, and of a sound mind. I declare my strength in you and resolve to conquer the giants that threaten my complete trust in you. Amen.

Day 21

*"I was ashamed to
ask the king for
soldiers and horsemen
to protect us from
enemies on the road,
because we had
told the king, "The
gracious hand of our
God is on everyone
who looks to him."
So we fasted and
petitioned our God
about this, and he
answered our prayer."*
—Ezra 8:22, 23

PRAYER:
*Jesus, I believe you
are able to do more
than I can ever ask or
imagine. I stand on
the same word I give
to others in their time
of need. You are my
provider, my help,
and my strength. I
trust you completely.
Amen.*

Anxiety dogged our steps as the deadline
drew closer without any sign of the
funds we expected. We dismissed all ideas of
borrowing from friends, and even if the bank
would approve a loan, we could not hope to
have the money on time.

One morning during prayer, God directed
me to Ezra. I immediately thought of all the
times I had encouraged others to trust in
God, Jehovah-Jireh, our provider. If I truly
believed, why was I panicking? I looked again
at Ezra's story. He was embarrassed to go back
to the king to ask for protection after boast-
ing how God protects those who trust in him.

At that moment, I decided to fast and pray
and simply trust God to be faithful. The
money came a full two days before the obli-
gation was to be met. It's so easy to encourage others to have faith, but how do we react
when we are in crisis? Do we complain to the
very ones whom we have told in the past of
the might and all-sufficiency of our God?
While our needs may not always be financial,
the principle is always the same. Sometimes
we should take our own advice and trust God
the way we encourage others to do. ❧

Faith may be imagined as a lofty plateau that allows us to stand and view the world through rose-colored glasses. Or faith may symbolize a sheltered harbor of dreams realized and wishes granted. Yet nothing in the Bible indicates that genuine faith in God precludes all difficulty or brings a sudden end to trouble. Instead, real faith contemplates all possible outcomes to the problem and still chooses to trust God. Faith that relies on visible evidence and frequent demonstrations may not even be faith at all.

The famous "Hall of Faith" in Hebrews 11 lists the great saints of old. None of these notable warriors saw the fulfillment of the things they so passionately believed, but they all died believing the prophecies would come to pass. Abraham and Sarah could not understand why God waited until, in Abraham's own words, "he was half dead" and his wife past childbearing age to give them a child. Still, they believed, and God came through with the beautiful child, Isaac.

Faith, then, becomes the road, not the destination. How we respond as we travel indicates the level of our confidence in God. Anyone can be full of faith and rejoice after prayers are answered, but it takes faith in God to be joyful when there seems to be no end to our distress. Faith in God causes us to say to the enemy, "I will not give in or compromise my stand because God is well able to deliver on his promises." ❦

Day 22

HAVE FAITH
IN GOD

"Have faith in God."
—Mark 11:22 KJV

PRAYER:
*Lord, your Word says
I cannot please you
except by faith.
Make me strong in
my resolve to walk
the road of faith
without being turned
aside by obstacles.
Amen.*

Day 23

HOLD ON
FOR THE BLESSING

"Then the man said, "Let me go, for it is daybreak." But Jacob replied, "I will not let you go unless you bless me." Then he blessed him there."
—Genesis 32:26, 29

PRAYER:
Heavenly Father, I wrestle daily with the guilt of my imperfections. Weighted down as I am with past mistakes, I sometimes miss your desire to erase the pain and cover me with blessings. I surrender to your grace and wait for your divine favor. Amen.

We sometimes grow tired and impatient with God and find ourselves wondering if our prayers will be answered. Faith evaporates as we conclude our request was not in the will of God anyway, and we just give up.

Jacob had a life-and-death need. He was going to see his brother Esau, whom he cheated out of his inheritance several years earlier. Jacob wrestled with the angel for a blessing, even as he wrestled inwardly with his feelings of guilt and remorse for all the dishonesty of his past. He knew only God could help him, and so nothing the angel said would make Jacob let go. The dawn drew closer, and profound weariness combined with the searing pain of his newly dislocated hip almost got the better of Jacob. The confrontation lasted so long that Jacob could no longer fight; instead he concentrated solely on just hanging on. He refused to let go until he received the help he so desperately needed.

God seldom gives us a time frame in which he will answer our prayers. He does promise, however, that he will always answer. We may wrestle or even get wounded as we wait for our blessing. When all is said and done, rest assured, like Jacob of old, God's blessing comes when we stop fighting and just hold on to him.

The hardest task for most of us is to do absolutely nothing. In fact, we pride ourselves on the number of things we can get done at the same time.

Imagine Moses, hemmed in by the Red Sea, inhospitable terrain, and Pharaoh's army. As the whole company seemed marked for death, God picks that time to tell Moses to do nothing.

"What do you mean, do nothing? After all, I am the leader and I'm at least partly responsible for the predicament we are in. I can't just stand here," Moses may have argued.

Nevertheless, standing there was exactly what he was expected to do. Whatever needed to be done, only God had the power to do it.

It's amazing what he accomplishes through and for us when we, in obedience, stand aside and let him work. God knows our limitations, and he knows when we need help. Furthermore, he will be right there to intervene on our behalf if we just ask. Beloved, sit still and leave the rest to him.✣

Day 24

YOU JUST NEED TO BE STILL

"The LORD will fight for you; you need only to be still."
—Exodus 14:14

PRAYER:
*Father, I get impatient and get in the way instead of allowing you to work.
I rest in you today believing you will fight—and win— my battles. Thank you for the victory.
Amen.*

Day 25

THE POWER OF FAITH

"We will worship and then we will come back to you."
—Genesis 22:5

PRAYER:
Father, I sometimes hold back on the things that are dear to me, afraid of losing my dream. Today, by faith, I release my life into your hands as a sacrifice and trust you to bring your promises to pass. Amen.

Pay close attention to the word "we." If Abraham was on his way to Mount Moriah to offer up Isaac as a sacrifice, how could he possibly tell his servants "we" (he and Isaac) are going up the mountain and will shortly return to you? God demanded a sacrifice—not an ordinary gift, but the very life of the child who was supposed to be the father of a great nation. Abraham looked beyond the reality of death and grabbed hold of faith. He was convinced that even if God had to resurrect Isaac, the original promise would still stand.

Faith goes beyond what we see, beyond what is usual in our given situation, surpassing the boundaries of human logic. We have no standard by which to measure God except his unchanging word. He tells us "[He] is not a man, that he should lie, nor a son of man, that he should change his mind. Does he speak and then not act? Does he promise and not fulfill?" (Num. 23:19). Our God has proven his constancy time and again.

As you might guess, Abraham's faith in God was justified. God never really wanted Isaac's life; rather, the request was a test of Abraham's loyalty. God just wanted to see if Abraham was willing to give up the most precious thing in his life. At the last moment, God provided a ram for the sacrifice and spared Isaac just as Abraham believed he would.

Do our faces reflect our faith? Hannah found herself in a pitiable condition. Being Eli's favorite wife had already raised the ire of the other wives. Added to that, Hannah could not have children. Finally the taunting and malice became so intense that Hannah stopped eating and abandoned herself to grief. She went to the temple and cried and begged God for a child.

Now, note the change. Hannah is rising from her knees. She is still in the temple. As yet there can be no evidence her prayer was answered. However, the depressed, grief-stricken woman who went in bears little resemblance to the one who comes out. Hannah rose from her knees with a smile, stopped fasting, and joyfully went on her journey home.

If, after we have taken our problem to the Lord, we remain sad, crying—and missing meals—our faith may remain disengaged. The knowledge of answered prayer brings peace and rest even before the object of our desire becomes visible. If we have to see it to believe it, then we are not acting in faith. Faith believes—because we are in Christ, the things we desire will be given to us according to his will, simply because we ask him. Jesus said, "Therefore I tell you, whatever you ask for in prayer, believe that you have received it, and it will be yours" (Mark 11:24).

Go ahead: pray, and then smile. ❧

Day 26

AFTER YOU PRAY, SMILE

"Then she went her way and ate something, and her face was no longer downcast."
—1 Samuel 1:18

PRAYER:
Lord Jesus, I give up my anxieties and lay my requests before you today. I praise you for answers, confident that you will do as you promise according to your divine will.
Amen.

Day 27

After the Rain

"Weeping may remain for a night, but rejoicing comes in the morning."
—Psalm 30:5

PRAYER:
Dear Father, I think of your promise that when I walk through the fire, it shall not burn me; when I go through the water, it shall not go over my head. Thank you for the assurance of joy at the end of every trial. Amen.

A succession of sunny days cannot begin to parallel the beauty of the sunshine following a rainy day. Possibly, the senses sharpened by the contrast of sun and rain are better able to appreciate warmth and light. At the end of the worst storm, the sun shines again, and the rainbow overarches the sky as a reminder of God's promise to us. One cannot savor a victory without knowing something about the agony of defeat. Likewise, joy can only be fully appreciated after the pangs of sorrow have done their worst.

Today, there may be angry clouds threatening the serenity of your life, or you may even be in the middle of a great storm. Do not despair. God is aware of your predicament and has promised to help and strengthen you. He accomplishes much in us and for his kingdom through adversity. Problems often drive us closer to him and make us listen to his voice like we never did before. We do not always relish the blinding showers, but we rejoice that God has promised after the showers that he will cause the Son of righteousness to bring us the joy of his presence. 🌸

Precious metals achieve their purity and beauty by going repeatedly through the fire. As the metal heats up, it softens, melts, and discloses the dross. The goldsmith or silversmith then carefully skims away and discards substances that rise to the top, leaving only what is pure. Unalloyed metals are also heated in order for them to be shaped and tempered as the artisan desires. In this process, steel will be taken from white-hot heat, only to be plunged in water, time and again.

Christ calls us his own special treasure, more precious than gold, silver, or any other ore. Is it any wonder, then, that he sometimes passes us through the floods of conflict or fiery trials? When we lose our luster, or our beauty becomes tarnished because of contamination by sin, our divine Artisan has no choice but to put us through the process again until his reflection is once more clearly defined in us. ❧

Day 28

THROUGH FIRE AND THROUGH WATER

"And whatever cannot withstand fire must be put through [the] water."
—Numbers 31:23

PRAYER:
Thank you, Heavenly Father, for the comfort of your presence through all the trials of life. Thank you for your unfailing tenderness as you make me more like you. Amen.

Day 29

FEAR NOT

"Do not be afraid or terrified for the LORD your God goes with you; he will never leave you nor forsake you."

—Deuteronomy 31:6

S aying "Don't be afraid" or "Everything is going to be all right" is definitely easier when we are consoling someone else. When we are challenged by dire financial reversals, a wayward child, a court battle that we are almost certain to lose, or an incurable disease, the words fall hollowly on our ears. Can it be we have faith to believe God for others and not for ourselves?

The Lord tells us: "Be not afraid or terrified, for I, God, am with you." Shouldn't it be enough that he who cannot lie has given us the promise of both his presence and his help? We have all, at some point or another, faced battles we are ill equipped to fight and forces we are powerless to repel. Our options are to panic, fret and succumb to despair, or rely on omnipotence to be our defense. Let us take God seriously. You can believe that what he did long ago, he will do today. Trust him and do not be afraid. ❦

Here the Scripture passage says [God] is the Rock, implying not comparison, but sovereignty. There is only one Rock because there is only one Lord God Almighty. We are reminded of the face off on Mount Carmel between the prophets of Baal and Elijah. Doubtless the Baal worshippers thought they would defeat Elijah by sheer force of numbers. It took but a short time for them to discover that God, by himself, constitutes a majority.

The Rock is eternally durable: "Before the mountains were born or you brought forth the earth and the world, from everlasting to everlasting you are God" (Ps. 90:2). He exists across the full spectrum of time and eternity. He is invincible, the only existing source of omnipotence. There is none other of whom it can be said that all power rests in their hands, in heaven or on earth.

God places that unshakable strength at our disposal today and invites us, in our weakness, to lean on him. ❦

Day 30

THE ROCK

"He is the Rock."
—Deuteronomy 32:4

PRAYER:
Dear Jesus,
I acknowledge you as
the one true God,
the Almighty.
I rely on your strength
today and always.
Amen.

Day 31

A PLACE OF REFUGE

"The eternal God is your refuge, and underneath are the everlasting arms."

—Deuteronomy 33:27

The Old Testament repeatedly mentions cities of refuge. In cases where one person unintentionally kills another, the offender has the option to run to a city of refuge for asylum. Every child of God has access to a place of refuge.

When we kill our joy by giving in to the hardships of life, there is a place we can run to and escape the wrathful hand of the enemy. We are reminded, "The name of the LORD is a strong tower; the righteous run to it and are safe." (Prov. 18:10). How do we run to a God we cannot see or touch? The Bible points the way. Pray or talk to God just as you would to anyone else. God created thought, language, and speech. There is nothing we can say to him that he does not understand.

Remember, also, that conversation goes both ways. So after praying or talking to God, we should listen to what he is saying to our spirit. We will know God is speaking because whatever he says to us will be in agreement with what the Bible teaches. Once we have received instruction, then we need to follow his direction. "God is our refuge and strength, an ever-present help in trouble" (Ps. 46:1). But just knowing this truth is not enough. We are only benefited if we go to him and act on what he instructs us to do. The world can offer us nothing that is 100 percent fail-safe. God does. He offers himself and all the power at his command. We know we can trust in him. 🌸

PRAYER:
*Heavenly Father,
I know I am protected
in you, and nothing
can remove me
from the safety of
your arms.
Amen.*

We all have something we fear above everything else. What do we do when dread removes itself from the realm of probability and becomes an all-too-tangible fact? What can we do when we are scrambling to pick up the pieces, all the time hoping we are in some horrible nightmare and will awaken soon?

Job must have treasured his health, his children, and his possessions. Not that he put them above God, but he gave them high value. Job devoutly hoped life would continue its even tenor. In less than a day he lost all that he had, and his worst fears became a reality. What was Job's response? He never blamed God, never gave up his faith, and never stopped believing that God would somehow make things right.

Some of us have yet to face our worst fears. The bottom may unexpectedly fall out of our tidy little worlds, leaving us spinning and disoriented in midair. Do we have to give up or fall apart? Hardly. God is greater than all our circumstances. Nothing takes him by surprise. He always has a plan. Like David, when our heart is faint we can find refuge in the one that is greater and stronger than we are.

After Job collided with his worst case scenario—and survived—the Bible says his later years were better than those of his youth (Job 42:12). When the devil does his worst, by faith we can reach for the grace of God and allow him to do his best for us. ❦

Day 32

WHEN FEARS COME TRUE

"What I feared has come upon me; what I dreaded has happened to me."
—Job 3:25

PRAYER:
*Dear Jesus,
I give you the burden
of my fears. I know
that, whatever comes,
your presence will
sustain and bring me
to the good years.
Amen.*

Day 33

"And a woman was there who had been subject to bleeding for twelve years, but no one could heal her."
—Luke 8:43

PRAYER:
Father, I have carried terrible burdens for many years. I have tried my own wisdom, the advice of others, all that the world recommends—and I am still sick. Today I give these burdens to you. Thank you for my healing and for accepting me as I am. Amen.

Medical science, home remedies, and repeated sin offerings had all been in vain. Money was gone. Her friends were no longer interested in her condition. To compound matters, the malady was obviously worsening. She knew in her heart that, in just a little while, the struggle would be over for good.

Unclean and excluded from the religious community, what would it matter if she went to see the controversial new prophet? Marshaling her fleeting courage, trying not to visualize the stoning that would surely follow if she was recognized in the crowd, she sallied forth. Just a little further, just a few more steps, and she would be close enough. Of course, she wouldn't speak to him. One of the people who were always with him might ask embarrassing questions. On the other hand, if she touched the part of his robe already considered unclean because of its contact with the dirt of the streets, what possible harm could that do?

Her limbs trembled with fatigue, and her breathing was now reduced to short, anxious gasps. Then, suddenly, she was pushed from behind, finding herself standing right behind Jesus. At the risk of being trampled, she knelt and quickly touched the very bottom of his robe. Life, precious life, began coursing through her body. For the first time in twelve years, she knew she was completely well.

Oh, no. Why did the prophet stop? And now he wanted to know who touched him. There was nowhere to hide and she couldn't lie, not when such love shone from his eyes. Trembling she stood before him. What? No words of condemnation? No remonstration for not coming to him sooner? No. Nothing but the voice of eternal consolation saying, "Go in peace."

Sometimes we find ourselves in seemingly dead-end situations, and we agonize at the prospect of long years of sameness and drudgery ahead. Even when we perceive our skills as imperfect and consider promotion unlikely or impossible, our situation is not hopeless. In fact, at this point God comes in. He is not governed by trends or profit margins. He sits transcendent, above all authority, sovereignly controlling the events of our lives.

David was as unqualified to be a king as anyone could possibly be. He had no experience of court life, no training in the art of statesmanship, and absolutely no idea how to be commander-in-chief over the nation of Israel. Yet he was God's best choice. In spite of what appear to be insurmountable odds, God can carve you out a niche and make room for you in more areas than you can even imagine. Are you willing to trust him? ❧

Day 34

THE GOD THAT MAKES ROOM

"Now the LORD has given us room and we will flourish in the land."
—Genesis 26:22

PRAYER:
Dear Jesus, today I pray for prosperity. Please open doors of opportunity for me in areas where I can best use my gifts and talents for you. Amen.

Day 35

A FATHER
WE CAN TRUST

*"Our Father
in Heaven."*
—Matthew 6:9

Tentatively, she dipped one toe and then one tiny foot into the water, only to run away screaming with each breaking wave. Who could blame her? Two years old and only a few feet tall, the ocean must have appeared formidable indeed. Minutes later her father waded in and beckoned to her, and everything changed. She no longer saw the vastness of the sea or felt fear from the waves as she dropped her bucket and shovel and went racing into his arms.

I couldn't help but think how much like that toddler we are. Life sometimes seems too big to handle. The problems are larger than our knowledge, the bills more than our resources, and every time we step forward, the waves come at us. But we have a Father— one who has the power to say to the waves, "Peace. Be still." Or, if he chooses, he may jump right into the water with us and, with his own body, bear the onslaught of the ocean.

God, the Creator, invites us to call him "Father." We can place our complete trust in his unfailing love. Our sea may remain just as big; yet, like that two-year-old, we can run to the safety of our Father's arms.

PRAYER:
*Dear Father, I run to
the safety of your
arms believing, you
are bigger than all the
waves in my life.
Thank you for your
peace today.
Amen.*

In Africa, each Christian native in a certain tribe had a secret place where he prayed. The path, leading to his place of prayer, was cleared by the native for his personal use. Whenever he was neglecting his prayer life, all that was needed to bring attention to this fact was the simple statement, "I see there is grass on your prayer trail."

—*William Cowper**

Day 36

GRASS ON THE
PRAYER TRAIL

"Faithful in prayer."
—Romans 12:12

Christ commands us to pray. He not only stresses the importance of frequent and fervent prayer, but all through his life he demonstrated how praying should be done. Before the start of his earthly ministry, he withdrew from the adulation surrounding the newly discovered Messiah for an extended quiet time with the Father. Later on, as his ministry grew, he still took time to slip away to recharge his spiritual energies in prayer. The Gospels give ample evidence of the effects of consistent prayer, so why is it so difficult for Christians to pray?

1. Prayer requires discipline. Like exercise, prayer seldom feels comfortable and easy when it is being done. No sooner than the habit is firmly established, however, the results become apparent. When we make the commitment to indulge in frequent, ardent prayer, God rewards us openly with his presence.
2. Effective prayer has its roots in repentance—not just a mumbled "I'm sorry," but an honest turning away from anything that could break our fellowship with God.

(continued next page)

Day 36

3. Prayer that gets results originates in hearts that are daily forgiving others even as Christ forgives them.
4. Last, and maybe the biggest hindrance, is simply time. Praying takes time. We can pray on the run all through the day, but deep communion with God demands a removal from the everyday pursuits and a total concentration on hearing the voice of the Father.

Jesus repeatedly spoke of his oneness with the Father, yet he fully appreciated the importance of times of solitary meditation. Keeping the grass off our prayer trail involves diligence and, sometimes, sacrifice. Hebrews 12:11 reminds us that, "No discipline seems pleasant at the time, but painful. Later on, however, it produces a harvest of righteousness and peace for those who have been trained by it." ❊

*Roy B. Zuck, The Speakers' Quote Book (Grand Rapids Michigan Kregel Publications, 1967).

PRAYER:
Draw me close to you, Father. Help me to pursue your presence and not just the gifts of your hands. Teach me to pray. Amen.

One would think that if anyone could really say they knew God, Moses could. He had seen and spoken to God face-to-face at the burning bush in the wilderness, and lived. Twice Moses went up to Sinai's summit, to receive the Ten Commandments. Surely he was as close to God as any human could be.

But Moses did not think so. Something about being close to God creates an insatiable hunger. The closer we get, the more we yearn for fellowship; the more we fellowship, the more desirable his company becomes. Moses pleaded for full disclosure. He never considered that a being powerful enough to set the mountain on fire might be a little hard for the human body to accommodate. Moses did not rest on past encounters or the glimpses of God's hand he had seen over the years. Instead, his very soul thirsted for something current: God's glory today.

No matter how long we live as Christians, we will never have complete understanding of the mighty God we serve. Let us continue to seek an intimate awareness of our Lord through daily times of prayer and communion with him through his Word. ❧

Day 37

SHOW ME YOUR GLORY

Then Moses said, "Now show me your glory."
—Exodus 33:18

PRAYER:
Lord, help me not to be so comfortable with where I have been that I cease to strive for fresh glimpses of your glory. Amen.

Day 38

NO PRAYER, NO POWER

One does not have to be a lifetime student of the life of Christ to discover that the power behind his ministry was his relationship with his Father. Repeatedly we see him leaving his disciples and the people and heading out alone to pray. Often these prayer vigils would occur very early in the morning, before the breaking of the dawn. Before performing miracles, he would lift his voice in supplication to his Father for help.

When we stop to think of Christ, one with the Father, Creator of all we see, literally God in the flesh—his habit of daily prayer becomes even more amazing. Why did Christ need to pray?

1. Prayer is conversation with God. Christ knew as long as he was earthbound, He needed to make sure his link to heaven remained intact.
2. Prayer reveals God's will. Christ had a timetable. All the Scriptures concerning him would be fulfilled, but in their perfect time without human help or coercion.
3. Christ led by example. If the perfect Son of God cultivated the presence of his father, can we afford to do less?

PRAYER:
*Dear Jesus,
your Word says your
Spirit gives us power
to live for you and
accomplish your work
here on earth.
Help me to seek your
presence in prayer as
I go through my day.
Amen.*

The thought of dying holds nothing but terror for many people, Christians and non-Christians alike. Some dread the loss of personhood, the thought of absolute oblivion, while others fear the dying process itself.

Paul, the apostle, affirms that to be absent from the body is to be present with the Lord (2 Cor. 5:6–8). What a thought! No sooner do we close the door to this life than we walk into the presence of God himself. The thief on the cross in unimaginable agony looked for mercy from one who, at first glance, seemed to be in the same lamentable predicament. Then, in a brief moment, the thief received new hope as Christ assured him, "Today you shall be with me in paradise." We can picture how the fear and anxiety lifted from this condemned man as death lost its finality and became a doorway into a life indescribably wonderful.

The Bible does not elaborate on the exact makeup of our bodies when we pass from death into everlasting life. However, we are reassured that we shall be like Christ, clothed in a body that will defy the ravages of time and eternity. This is the blessed hope of the believer—not death and oblivion or endless cycles of repeating the same mistakes, but a glorious opportunity to be alive with Christ forever. 🍂

Day 39

A GOOD WAY TO DIE

"Let me die the death of the righteous, and may my end be like theirs!"
—Numbers 23:10

PRAYER:
*Lord Jesus,
because of you we
have the glorious hope
of everlasting life.
Help me to share the
good news with
someone today.
Amen.*

Day 40

*"Joshua said to
the LORD in the
presence of Israel:
"O sun, stand still
over Gibeon,
O moon, over the
valley of Aijalon."
So the sun stood still,
and the moon
stopped."*
—Joshua 10:12, 13

PRAYER:
*Father, through the
power you have given
to all who believe in
you, I speak victory
over the enemy of
my soul. I will be
victorious in my
life—physically,
emotionally, finan-
cially, and spiritually.
Thank you, Lord.
Amen.*

We frequently underestimate the inherent power of the spoken word, even though God tells us the "Tongue has the power of life and death" (Prov. 18:21), and that we are acquitted or condemned by our words (Matt. 12:37).

Joshua was in the middle of a battle, with victory in sight. All he needed was a few more hours of daylight to pursue his advantage. Instead of moaning about the waning light, Joshua grabbed his faith with both hands and spoke an earth-stopping word. Joshua commanded the sun and moon to stop moving, and God brought the forces of nature in obedience to the faith Joshua expressed.

Today our battles may not be as literal. Our enemy may be attitudes, fear, or depression. Speak to it. Declare your position as a child of God and refuse to be defeated by the adversary. Less energy is needed to speak positively than to speak words that weaken and destroy our confidence in God. Speak victory. ❦

When King Hezekiah received Sennacherib's blasphemous letter, he responded in a peculiar way. He did not call for his counselors or generals to map out a defense strategy, nor did he call for a scribe to dictate a response. Rather, he read the letter, then took it to the temple and spread it out upon the altar before the Lord.

We sometimes waste a lot of time and energy by going to the wrong people with our problems. We tend to talk to those who feed our anger and make us more resentful and unforgiving toward the ones who wronged us. At other times, we dump our grief on shoulders already stooped from the weight of their own burdens, and leave them more depressed than ever.

Maybe we should take a leaf from Hezekiah's book and talk to someone who can really do something about what ails us. Before we pick up the phone to tell a friend what just happened or complain about all the misfortune dogging our steps, take the problem to Jesus and spread it out before him. As the song says,

> Tell it to Jesus, tell it to Jesus
> He is a friend that's well known
> We have no other such a friend or
>   brother
> Tell it to Jesus alone.*

*"Tell It to Jesus" by Jeremiah E. Rankin (1828–1904) and Edmund S. Lorenz (1854–1942).

Day 41

TALK TO THE
RIGHT PERSON

"Hezekiah received the letter from the messengers and read it. Then he went up to the temple of the LORD and spread it out before the LORD."
—2 Kings 19:14

PRAYER:
*Dear Jesus,
I bring you my problems today,
all the concerns of my heart, everything that makes me uncomfortable or unhappy. I give you my despair and accept the hope and strength you alone can give.
Amen.*

Day 42

A CALL TO PRAYER

"If my people, who are called by my name, will humble themselves and pray and seek my face and turn from their wicked ways, then will I hear from heaven and will forgive their sin and heal their land."

—2 Chronicles 7:14

PRAYER:
*Dear Jesus, so often I focus on things, on what others have done or should do, and I forget your purpose for me. I repent of my own failings and pray for a revival in my heart, my country, and my world.
Amen.*

We watch in growing dismay as drugs, violence, and sexual immorality continue to escalate, and we conclude that our world needs an awakening. As we read the Bible, we find out that God says whatever is wrong with the nations can be rectified if his people pray. Note the emphasis is not on sinners repenting, but rather on the people of God developing a hunger for him.

When Christians pray and seek after God, they begin to take him at his word and hate sin like he does. When believers decide to turn away from everything that hurts the Holy Spirit, God promises he will hear from heaven and send a glorious change to our world. As we who are called the church begin to demonstrate Christ's character, sinners will be attracted to following him. For this reason he told us to let our lights shine bright enough that others may be drawn to glorify him.

Are we really praying for God's will to be done in our lives and in the world at large? As one preacher aptly puts it, "God does not revive congregations, but individuals." Are we open enough to the voice of God that he can wake us up early or keep us up late to intercede for the need of others? The formula for spiritual awakening is not given to unbelievers; rather, the message is addressed to us, his people. When we humble ourselves—devoting ourselves to seeking the face rather than the hand of God—the healing will come. ❧

Most people think not being among the governing body of society means being without the means to effect significant change. God, on the other hand, takes an entirely different viewpoint. He does not belittle or negate the power of one solitary prayer. In fact, the Bible gives ample evidence of the very course of nature being altered because one person dared to pray.

Elijah, in response to Ahab and Jezebel's wickedness, prayed the rain would stop falling, and it did for a whole three and a half years. Joshua prayed the sun would stand still in order to secure victory, and daylight was sustained. One prayer by Joseph for the correct interpretation of Pharaoh's dream resulted in the salvation of Egypt and her neighboring countries. The stories continue. In Ezekiel's day, God searched for just one person to intercede on Jerusalem's behalf so destruction of the city could be averted. A force of one, in prayer, can move the heart of God and bring about changes we cannot even begin to imagine.

Day 43

A Force of One

"I looked for a man among them who would build up the wall and stand before me in the gap on behalf of the land so I would not have to destroy it, but I found none."
—Ezekiel 22:30

PRAYER:
Father, I pray our nation will awaken to your sovereignty; I pray for peace at home and in foreign lands; I pray that your rule and reign will be established in our hearts and lives. Amen.

Day 44

PRAYING
FOR PASTORS

*"Brother,
pray for us."*
—1 Thessalonians 5:25

Miriam sat at the foot of the bed looking at the top of Taylor's head as he said his prayers. She yawned as he began the list of "and blesses," hoping his memory would give out before she fell asleep. ". . . and bless Daddy, and Mommy, and Ga-ma, and Patta Bwown (Pastor Brown) and, and Amen." Tears filled Miriam's eyes as she kissed her son and tucked his blankets around him.

Paul, before he ended his first letter to the church in Thessalonica, made one simple request: "Pray for us." Not only did he ask them, but throughout his letters we see him asking for others to pray that boldness, opportunity to minister, and even traveling mercies be given to him.

We pray for people we care about, for the ones who occupy our thoughts and affections. We spend time in prayer for those whom we consider in need of divine help. Do pastors fit any of these categories? The prayer of a little child reminds us to pray for pastors, our spiritual leaders, and all those who labor in the work of the ministry. 🌿

PRAYER:
*Dear Jesus, I pray for
pastors, Christian
leaders, and all who
bring others to
know you as Savior.
I pray especially for
missionaries who have
left home and friends
to serve you in foreign
lands. Thank you for
their sacrifice and
godly example.
Amen.*

The Prophet—The description of Jonah as "the son of Amittai" gives us his prophetic lineage. In other words, Jonah was not pretending to be called of God; he was a genuine prophet, with a genuine grievance against the Ninevites. He wanted to see them punished. Therefore, when God gave Jonah the message, instead of going east as the command indicated, he went far west. Jonah attempted to obey only when his own life was in danger. Such is the measure of God's mercy that He didn't allow the prophet to die in disobedience, but gave him another opportunity to deliver the message to Nineveh.

The People—No sooner had Jonah delivered his message than the king of Nineveh called a nationwide fast and cried out to God for mercy. Once again, God proved his love will always outrun his justice, and the people of Nineveh were spared.

Does it matter what sin we have committed or how long we have walked contrary to God's laws? Does it matter if we are the preacher with a grudge, or if we once walked with him but now no longer call him Lord? No, it does not matter. God promises us his mercy and abundant pardon when we turn to him. 🌱

Day 45

GOD OF THE
SECOND CHANCE

*"From inside the fish
Jonah prayed."*
—Jonah 2:1

*"When God saw how
they turned from their
evil ways he did not
bring upon them the
destruction he had
threatened."*
—Jonah 3:10

PRAYER:
*Dear Jesus, I do not
understand why you
continue to give
second chances, but
I'm grateful for your
forgiveness today and
all through my life.
Amen.*

Day 46

RESTRAINING LOVE

"When Israel was a child, I loved him."
—Hosea 11:1

God is recounting all he did for his people to demonstrate his great love. He begins with an endearing picture of a father teaching his child to walk and continues on with his faithful provision for their every need. As the chapter progresses, God bares his soul and appears less like a cold, distant being and more like a husband and father grieving over those he loves. His justice cries out for vengeance as his care is repeatedly spurned. The Israelites turn to the people and nations around them for support, instead of to the one who so earnestly loves them.

God sees around him the ruins of nations that turned their backs on him, and compassion overcomes holy jealously. "How can I give you up, how can I make you like Adamah and Zeboim?" he asks (Hosea 11:8). Jesus reiterates the Father's love for sinners when he says, "For God so loved the world that he gave his one and only Son, that whoever believes in him shall not perish but have eternal life" (John 3:16).

Why do we not die the moment we sin? Why are the perpetrators of dastardly crimes against humanity allowed to live? Certainly not because of justice, but mercy. We stand forgiven in the presence of grace only because of God's restraining love. He does not desire that sinners die in their sins or that his children be cut off in a state of rebellion. He longs to take our hand again and teach us to walk in love and fellowship with him. 🌿

PRAYER:
O love that will not let me go
I rest my weary soul in thee
I give thee back the life I owe
That in life's ocean depths it's flow
May richer fuller be.*
Amen.

*"Oh Love That Will Not Let Me Go" by George Matheson (1842–1906) and Albert L Peace (1844–1912).

Until we are faced with situations beyond our limited capabilities, we cannot fully appreciate the importance of these aspects of God's personality. As long as we feel that we can resolve our problems, there's a tendency to run around in circles, mostly getting in the way of what God really wants to do on our behalf. He describes himself as a refuge or hiding place for all those who are in trouble. There is never a danger so threatening or terror so all consuming that we cannot go to Christ and hide in him. Not only is he a haven, he is also our strength.

Who among us can deny being brought to the end of human endurance by some adversity? Yet we derive comfort in knowing that when our strength is at its lowest ebb, God always steps in. Remember these truths when carefully laid plans go awry and your house of dreams stands in imminent danger of collapse. God, our help, stands available to do the impossible so we may accomplish the unthinkable.

*Psalm 20:7

Day 47

REFUGE, STRENGTH
AND HELP

*"God is our refuge
and strength, an
ever-present help
in trouble."*
—Psalm 46:1

PRAYER:
*My Father, like the
psalmist I affirm that
some people trust in
chariots and some in
horses, but [I] will
remember the name of
the Lord [my] God.*
Thank you for always
being on my side.
Amen.*

Day 48

*"The angel of the
LORD encamps
around those who
fear Him, and he
delivers them."*
—Psalm 34:7

We sat under the picnic shed watching the rain falling in unbroken sheets from the darkened sky. Even with umbrellas, we were drenched as we made the short dash to the car. Before us the road curved and dipped as it snaked its way down the mountainside. The long trail of oil left by eighteen-wheelers mixed with the warm summer rain made the surface slick as sealskin.

As we neared a particularly treacherous curve, the driver braked, and the car skidded. Gathering momentum, it rolled onto the gravelly shoulder, just skimming the lip of an almost bottomless ravine. Moments later the front tires cleared the shoulder and slammed sideways into a light post. Head-on would have been fatal for the front passenger and maybe the driver. Missing the light post would have undoubtedly guaranteed a headlong descent to certain death in the valley below. A policeman viewing the wreck asked, "Did you pray this morning?" Thank God, we had.

We often read the Bible or sing words of a song without ever grasping the full implications of what we are saying. Even when we ask for protection during the course of a day, the request is sometimes more ritual than inner conviction that without divine aid, our lives may be forfeited. Our prayers are important. God waits to hear us pray and hastens to send angels to attend us when we need them the most. 🌿

PRAYER:
*God, thank you
for angelic hosts
guarding all those
who believe in you.
We give back our lives
as a sacrifice to you.
Amen.*

Picture Moses looking in all directions. Then, convinced the Egyptian was entirely at his mercy, he struck the fatal blow. Did Moses actually look in all directions? No, he did not look up.

Not looking up or giving recognition to God, who is aware of all we do, is still an all-too-frequent mistake. We are concerned about what those around us may say. We expend energy making sure we remain in a favorable light before our peers. Isaiah reminds us "He [the LORD] is the one [we] are to fear, he is the one [we] are to dread" (Isa. 8:13). Jesus, speaking to the disciples says, "Do not be afraid of those who kill the body but cannot kill the soul. Rather, be afraid of the One who can destroy both soul and body in hell" (Matt. 10:28).

Today, can we resolve to look up and think about God first? After all, he sees us no matter where we are or what we do. In the long run, his opinion is the only one that matters.

Day 49

GOD ALWAYS SEES ME

Moses glanced this way and that and [saw] no one.
—Exodus 2:12

PRAYER:
Father, sometimes I forget to try to please you before pleasing others. Remind me to be conscious of the One who always sees me. Amen.

Day 50

PERFECT KNOWLEDGE

"For you know your servant, O Sovereign LORD."
—2 Samuel 7:20

God never misunderstands—not our motives, words, or actions. No matter how much dissonance exists between our thoughts and the direction we pursue, God still understands. You may be struggling to express with pristine clarity your love for the Master. You may wonder why it is so difficult to talk to those closest to you about your faith in Christ as Savior. Jesus knows your love, hears your desire, and blesses every stammering effort.

Is there an area of your life where light has never penetrated, something you blush to mention even in prayer? God already knows. He sees your shame and longs to take away your burden. When loneliness causes us to pantomime real life, laughing through hidden tears of anguish, God hears. Does this change his opinion of us? Not in the least. He does not distance himself from our pain. Instead, he calls us to his bosom and offers forgiveness, grace, and unconditional love. Then he graciously opens the way that we may know him.

PRAYER:
Heavenly Father, I voluntarily expose all the secret areas of my life to you. Make me clean in your sight, and help me to live the love I feel for you in my heart. Amen.

We are seldom sympathetic when we talk about the children of Israel in the wilderness as they grumbled against God. From the safe distance of thousands of years later, we pass judgment and condemn them for their faithlessness. The same treatment is given to the people of Jesus' day. We are convinced we would have recognized Christ and followed him as Messiah.

Would we really? With all the evidence of both Old and New Testaments behind us, we still doubt. Every one of us falls prey to anxiety when "Red Sea" situations threaten our well-being. Yet, in the middle of our unbelief, one thing remains true: God is never at a loss for a way to bring about our deliverance. His hands are not too short; his mercy reaches us wherever we are. In fact, he has a reputation for hearing before we call and answering our request before we ask (Isa. 65:24).

Are you going through a faith-stretching exercise? God's arm is long enough to reach you. The God of the Bible hasn't changed. He is still able. ❦

Day 51

GOD IS STILL ABLE

"Is the LORD's arm too short?"
—Numbers 11:23

PRAYER:
Father, thank you for your absolute dependability.
I rejoice that you are in absolute control of your world and of my life.
Amen.

Day 52

*"Fight the good fight
of the faith."*
—1 Timothy 6:12

From the moment of birth until the day we die, we are engaged in warfare. After we become Christians, the battle intensifies as we align ourselves against the enemy of our souls. Warfare is not for a few special people. Rather, it is the eternal battle of good versus evil as the devil attempts to exercise lordship over God's creation. As in any other war, the conflict can sometimes be overwhelming as the enemy gains the advantage. But even in those times, we can rejoice because Jesus guarantees us victory in the end.

We are instructed to put on the full armor of God in order to take our stand against the schemes of the evil one (Eph. 6:11). The strategies vary, and the attacks may originate from different directions; only his desire to destroy remains the same. After we make sure we have all our protective gear in place, we are expected to pray—and not only for our strength or the good of the soldiers we see around us. Intercede for God's army everywhere. Then one day, like the apostle Paul, we too will say we have fought a good fight, finished the race, and kept the faith. Like Paul, we shall receive a crown. ❦

PRAYER:
*Dear Jesus,
today I put on the
helmet of salvation,
the breastplate of
righteousness, the
shield of faith, and the
sword of the Spirit.
I wear the belt of
truth, the shoes of
peace, and a mantle
of prayer as protection
against the enemy.
Amen.*

Traditions are hard to break. Old religious customs representing the bedrock of our cultural identity are even harder to give up. Many people coming into Christianity from other religions find it difficult to give up former beliefs. Sometimes newcomers incorporate elements of the old system into their new life. In time, a hybrid emerges with shadings of both faiths, and a complete commitment to Christ is not realized. Is Christ enough? Is the God of the universe worth risking everything for?

If this Christ is all he says he is, then we do not need to hedge our bets by continuing other religious practices as well. We are Christians because we admitted the inadequacy of any other god to save us or give us eternal life. A secret adherence to charms or a dependence on astrology to determine the course of our lives implies somehow that God is incapable of caring for us in the physical realm.

Being a Christian means being reborn. Our whole lifestyle changes as we give up our old, useless practices and live life based on complete trust in Christ—for everything.

Besides, the Bible reminds us that God is a jealous God, one who will not share his glory. He is, however, willing to honor those who honor him. What greater honor can we give him than to renounce all other gods and completely trust him?

Day 53

DIVIDED LOYALTY

"Nevertheless, each national group made its own gods. They worshiped the LORD, but they also served their own gods."
—2 Kings 17:29, 33

PRAYER:
*My Father,
thank you for the
gift of salvation and
everlasting life.
I promise to worship
you and to see my
future only in light
of your word.*
Amen.

Day 54

READY
FOR ANYTHING

*"They were
brave warriors,
ready for battle."*
—1 Chronicles 12:8

PRAYER:
*Almighty God,
today I put on your
full protection. I pray
for the protection of
my loved ones, the
armed forces, and
your soldiers all over
the world. I open my
heart to the voice
of your Holy Spirit.
Help me to
respond quickly to
your commands.
Amen.*

A picture of Christianity far removed from the nonchalant "I'm o.k., you're o.k." philosophy the world espouses is presented in Ephesians 6. The truth is that we are locked in mortal combat with the enemy, and only our special weaponry guarantees our survival. How do we become battle ready?

First, by knowing the enemy—not the people who annoy or harass us, but the arch-enemy of God himself, Satan. "For we wrestle not against flesh and blood, but against principalities, against powers." (Eph. 6:12, KJV).

Second, by accepting and equipping ourselves with the weapons provided for our use. This is accomplished by putting on the whole armor of God—not just the portions we like, but the full gear as all the pieces work together for our protection and ultimate victory. Our headgear reflects changed thinking by minds made new in Christ. We protect our hearts, the seat of our emotions and wellspring of our life.

Right living is used to harness our emotions so we do not run after our own desires and fall into sin. The loins are supported by truth, and our feet are covered with the gospel of peace. Faith, by its very nature, is something unseen. Is it any wonder that God gives us the shield of faith to block the fiery darts of the enemy? He can throw all he has at us, but he never knows when faith is going to rise up and render his attacks powerless.

Lastly, the Word of God is our sword. Though prayer is not given directly as part of the armor, its value cannot be overemphasized. No army can effectively fight without maintaining communication with its commanding officers. Prayer links us to the mind of God and enables us to remain in battle formation. The only unprotected part of our body is our back. Good soldiers don't run. ❦

Joshua moved his forces to just outside the walls of Jericho in preparation for attacking the city. With sentries securing the perimeter of the camp, he was unprepared to be accosted by a stranger with a drawn sword. Joshua quickly recovered himself and demanded of the stranger whether he was friend or foe. To his surprise the stranger answered, "Neither, but as commander of the army of the LORD I have now come." Joshua was then told to take off his sandals, as where he stood was now holy ground (Josh. 5:15).

As the commander of the army of the Lord or the Lord God of Hosts, Christ is uniquely equipped to not only map out battle strategies, but to ensure we are victorious in whatever we do. He anticipates the difficulties and always provides a way of escape. God does not depend on human wisdom, strength, or skill to carry out his plans. The toughest battle only needs the intervention of the commander.

Not surprisingly, the commander had a radically different plan than Joshua had in mind. No covert operation, no systematic infiltration of the enemy's camp, in fact, no fighting at all. Instead, much to the army's surprise, the city of Jericho was leveled by a march and a well-timed shout. We may be going about our battles the wrong way using so-called tried and true methods. The commander has a winning strategy if we will listen to him.

Day 55

THE DIVINE COMMANDER

"As Commander of the army of the LORD I have now come."
—Joshua 5:14

PRAYER:
Divine Commander, I submit my plans to you. The ways I have tried have either failed or brought success at a very high price. Today I listen and purpose to follow where you lead. Amen.

Day 56

*"The men of
Ephraim, though
armed with bows,
turned back on the
day of battle."*
—Psalm 78:9

A n old cliché says that self-preservation is the first law. However, focusing only on saving our lives can cause us to abandon our faith and confidence in God. An entire company of soldiers forgot God's deliverance from Pharaoh's bondage. The ample provision as they journeyed through the wilderness disappeared in one bright flash of terror. Instead of taking comfort in past victories when they were equally outnumbered yet triumphed, the soldiers ran, leaving defenseless the people they were sworn to protect.

When we refuse to strike a blow against the adversary, we are expressing doubt in one of the following areas: the ability of our leader, the efficacy of our weapons, or the possibility of victory. We are people of faith and should not be readily influenced by how things appear. Christ is the conquering lion of the tribe of Judah. He remains victorious over death, hell, and the grave, and it is he that goes before us.

May God help us today to be brave and face down the enemy. Like Shammah, may we take our stand in the middle of our [battle] field and defend it until God gives us the victory (2 Sam. 23:12). 🌸

PRAYER:
*Lord, I draw courage
from your Spirit
that gives me strength
in every trial.
Amen.*

et us look back at how far we have come. The apostle Paul reminds that us we were lost in sin without God in the world, but in due time, Christ died for us (Rom. 5:6). In other words, we had no means of saving ourselves and no will to live godly lives if, by chance, we stumbled onto the truth. We were described as aliens, foreigners, and idolaters who were just as happy worshiping the creation or inanimate objects of our own design.

Christ entered our hopelessness and said, "I have loved you with an everlasting love" (Jer. 31:3). Suddenly, we who were nameless and not considered a nation are now children of God, co-inheritors with Christ of all the riches of the Father. He brought us out of sin and emptiness into his glorious kingdom.

Still, the culmination is yet to come. We have Christ's own word that he is preparing a place for us, and he will come again to receive us to live with him forever (John 14:2, 3).

Day 57

BROUGHT OUT, TO BE BROUGHT IN

"But he brought us out from there to bring us in and give us the land."
—Deuteronomy 6:23

PRAYER:
Heavenly Father, thank you for bringing me out of sin and adopting me into your family. I pledge my life to the honor and glory of your kingdom. Amen.

Day 58

SEDUCED BY
APPEARANCES

*"The men of
Israel sampled their
provisions but did
not inquire of
the LORD."*
—Joshua 9:14

PRAYER:
*Father, I ask your
wisdom for all the
decisions I must make
during the course of
this day. Help me not
to give in to pressure
and decide hastily or
to rely only on my
own skill or wisdom.
Help me make right
choices. Amen.*

The men, their supplies, and their clothing looked travel-worn. Although they did not say specifically what country they were from, their appearance gave the impression they came from a great distance. No one wondered why, as ambassadors, they took no extra clothing and no servants to attend them on their journey. Maybe the elders were flattered that they, who were former slaves, had grown to such power; a country they never even heard of wanted to be their ally. Whatever the reason, they skipped a vitally important step in their decision-making process. They forgot to ask God if an alliance was acceptable to him. Consequently, Israel locked itself into a treaty with the very people God wanted them to destroy.

Nothing can be more misleading than appearances. Humans look at outward beauty or become swept away on an emotional tide by pleasant-sounding words. God, on the other hand, looks at the heart. Unlike Joshua, we may find we are unable to modify the results of our bad decisions, and we may even suffer great loss in the end.

God gives us the option to come to him and ask for direction in our day-to-day choices. We are exhorted to "Trust in the LORD with all [our] heart[s] and lean not on [our] own understanding, in all [our] ways acknowledge him, and he will make [our] paths straight" (Prov. 3:5, 6). ❀

Wouldn't it be great if we could look forward to a no-bumps-in-the-road, problem-free Christian life? Then we could just stroll along Glory Avenue to heaven. Wow! What a dream. And that's really all it is. The reality is somewhat different. Christianity is described as a fight, a battle, a narrow road, and a cross, among other things. Every description bears the connotation of suffering or hardship.

Fortunately, no time limit is placed on when we should complete the race. Have you ever watched a marathon and noticed that long after the winner is announced, people still continue to push across the finish line? Why? They were not running to be first, but to finish the race.

It doesn't matter if our spirits become weary and we feel we lack the strength to continue. God is not concerned that others who started the race after us are running faster or better than we are. Instead, we can, like the apostle Paul, determine to forget everything else and go for the gold, the crown of life promised to all those who cross the finish line. ✳

Day 59

DON'T STOP NOW

"Gideon and his three hundred men, exhausted yet keeping up the pursuit, came to the Jordan and crossed it."
—Judges 8:4

PRAYER:
*Dear Lord Jesus,
I pledge my allegiance
to you again.
I promise to be
faithful to you, no
matter how hard the
road becomes or how
intense the struggle.
I depend on your
unfailing strength.
Amen.*

Day 60

*"Then the LORD
opened the servant's
eyes, and he looked
and saw the hills
full of horses and
chariots of fire all
around Elisha."*
—2 Kings 6:17

When unfriendly circumstances hem us in, powerlessness and fear become dominant emotions. We begin bracing ourselves for the disaster we are certain will occur. Gehazi, Elisha's servant, must have felt somewhat like that when he awakened and found the city under siege. We can identify with his panic as he runs back to the prophet and asks, "What shall we do?" We can also imagine his surprise when Elisha told him not to worry, as the forces with them outnumbered those camped about the city. Gehazi had no idea what Elisha was talking about. Seeing the servant's confusion, the prophet prayed, "LORD, open his eyes." Relief flooded Gehazi, sweeping doubts and fears aside as he finally saw God's army covering the hillside, stretching as far as the eye could see.

Panic disappeared when Gehazi's eyes became open to the power of God and the completeness of his protection. Today our safety is just as sure. "The angel of the LORD encamps around those who fear him, and he delivers them" (Psalm 34:7). It is possible, like Gehazi, we need our eyes divinely opened to the truth of how comprehensively covered we are. ❧

PRAYER:
*Dear Jesus,
I am grateful for
your protection as
I go through my days.
Open my eyes
to the completeness
of your care.
Amen.*

Going to friends or acquaintances with our innermost fears and anxieties often results in being ignored or made to feel foolish. We may even hear that we should know better and that nothing is really wrong with us. So, we paint on a smile, nod in agreement, and pretend everything is all right.

How different is our Lord's approach! When we go to him, he treats us like children afraid of the dark. He comes into our situation, shines the light of his presence around us, and dispels our fears. Additionally, like the door to the parents' room left open during the night for the comfort of the tearful child, he whispers he will never leave or forsake us. If we are still in distress, he leaves with us the blessed Holy Spirit to ensure our rest. ❧

*Psalm 23

Day 61

DELIVERED
FROM FEAR

*"I sought the LORD,
and he answered me;
he delivered me from
all my fears."*
—Psalm 34:4

PRAYER:
*The LORD is my
shepherd, I shall not be
in want. He makes me
lie down in green
pastures, he leads me
beside the quiet waters,
he restores my soul. He
guides me in paths of
righteousness for his
name's sake. Even,
though I walk through
the valley of the shadow
of death, I will fear no
evil, for you are with
me; your rod and your
staff, they comfort me.
You prepare a table
before me in the presence
of my enemies. You
anoint my head with oil;
my cup overflows. Surely
goodness and love will
follow me all the days of
my life, and I will dwell
in the house of the
LORD forever.*
Amen.

Day 62

SET APART

"Now, who is willing to consecrate himself today to the LORD?"
—1 Chronicles 29:5

PRAYER:
*Dear Jesus,
you have kept all your
promises to me, and
I want to be just as
true to you. I renew
my vow to be your
disciple and to be
set apart to
serve you alone.
Amen.*

When we came to Christ and asked him to be our Savior, we also promised Him we would dedicate our lives to him. We stated our commitment to Christ in different ways, yet our words must have been similar to the lyrics of the hymn "I Surrender All":

All to Jesus I surrender
All to Him I freely give
I will ever love and trust Him
In His presence daily live.*

This is a lifetime commitment with no clauses providing an out when problems overtake us, or when disillusionment rears its ugly head. Nothing in this contract implies that our service to God will depend on how we are treated by others or on how the people around us respond to God's laws. Voluntarily, we said, "I surrender," thereby setting ourselves apart for his service.

Timothy says we are all vessels in the Master's house, and he decides what our function will be (2 Tim. 2:20, 21). If we keep ourselves from sin, we can be used to great honor by the Lord. Though vessels sometimes fall and are broken, the pieces are never discarded. God loves us so much he picks us up, repairs or remolds us, and gives us a whole new life in him.

When doubts and bitterness cause us to become misshapen, the Master refashions us and redirects us until his will is once again revealed in our lives. The road we travel is littered with broken promises and abandoned vows. But God wants to work through us to show to the world it is possible and even desirable to live a life dedicated to his service.

*Judson W. Van Venter (1855–1939), Winfield S. Weden (1847–1908).

No doubt many of the younger generation felt Joshua was terribly old-fashioned. Imagine: he still clung to the old laws, including the practice of not intermarrying with the surrounding nations, even after the Israelites were established in Canaan. After all, that law was issued over forty years ago, and all the people who came out of Egypt (except Caleb and Joshua) were dead. Why did they still bother with the old customs anyway?

Thousands of years have passed since Jesus lived and walked on earth. As we demonstrate and talk about the truth of his teachings, we are often accused of being out of touch with cultural norms. This accusation, however, should not change our stance.

Passing years do not alter the relevance of the Bible. God is still holy, the devil is still virulently evil, and sin will ultimately be punished. Let us ask God for grace and wisdom to go against the tide of popular opinion. If necessary, we should be able to say with unshakeable determination, "I will serve the Lord." ✾

Day 63

GOING AGAINST THE ODDS

"But as for me and my household, we will serve the LORD."
—Joshua 24:15

PRAYER:
Lord Jesus, you have shown me by your life what it means to be unpopular for speaking the truth yet staying the course in the Father's name. I want to be as unwavering in my service to you. Amen.

Day 64

THE BLOOD THAT CLEANSES

"The blood of Jesus, [God's] Son, purifies us from all sin."
—1 John 1:7

I never understood why Miss Lynn took a liking to me. However, shortly after we met she decided we were friends. On a fairly regular basis, she started bringing me home-grown vegetables wrapped in dirty brown paper. Miss Lynn would sometimes stick out a grubby hand and demand a handshake. She would then give her toothless grin and say, "The only thing soap and water can't wash clean is a dirty conscience."

What an amazing truth! Our own "washing" of our consciences by doing good works or by being persons of good moral character, all fall short of what God requires. We could only save ourselves if we could be as good and pure as God himself, and the Scripture already says we all have sinned. Thank God, there is hope! Christ died for our sins and his sacrifice on Calvary washes away every stain. All we need to do is admit we are sinners, be sorry for our sins, and turn away from them. When we accept his death on our behalf, confess our sins, and believe he truly forgives all who come to him, we can say we are indeed clean. ❦

PRAYER:
*Dear Jesus,
I know there was
nothing I could do to
save myself or be
perfect in your sight.
Thank you for your
blood that takes
away my sin.
Amen.*

With the sudden rebirth of interest in all things prophetic, and so many people claiming to have a word from the Lord, some Christians have become lazy. Some people today will travel miles or even go to the considerable expense of plane fare and hotel accommodations to receive a word. The idea of spending time alone in prayer until God speaks is almost outdated.

Hearing from God is a privilege open to every believer. As God explains it, the only time he interrupts our communication with him is when there is sin in our hearts (Ps. 66: 18). Rebekah is hardly the example that comes to mind when we think of a woman of extreme piety. Yet, when she became conscious of the extraordinary events taking place in her womb, she went to God directly to find out the reason behind the problem.

We need no special words or superior knowledge of the Bible to talk to God. Just there, right where you are, in your own words, you can talk to him, and because you are his child, he will answer. Will you take the time and go to him today? ❧

Day 65

FIND OUT FOR YOURSELF

"Why is this happening to me?"
So she went to inquire of the LORD."
—Genesis 25:22

PRAYER:
My Father in heaven,
I come to you today.
I want to hear your
voice, to follow
your direction.
Lead me I pray.
Amen.

Day 66

A DAILY DENIAL

"If anyone would come after me, he must deny himself and take up his cross daily and follow me."
—Luke 9:23

W hy daily? Wouldn't it be easier to simply make a lifetime vow to Christ and never think about it again? That way one could have the comfort of being a child of God without exerting any conscious effort. Doubtless such a life would be easier for us, but it would do nothing to maintain or deepen our relationship with God.

Each day is lived on its own merits, and our daily trials and triumphs differ, as does our response to each situation. Every day we are required to make a deliberate decision whether or not we will live for Christ in all we do. There will never be a day when our selfish desires will not make war and try to overpower the spirit of God in us.

Equally, each day as Christians, we are given the challenge to take up our cross— that is, to take a stand in some way or the other against the world's system. Christianity cannot be experienced on cruise control. Will you take up your cross today and follow the Master?

PRAYER:
Heavenly Father, denying the clamor of my own nature is just impossible without your help. Give me the inner strength of your Holy Spirit to follow willingly until I am made anew in your image. Amen.

There was a man named Micah, an Israelite of the tribe of Ephraim. He knew the law and the stipulations against idolatry, and he also knew God had chosen Shiloh as the place to worship. Micah decided he would not go to Shiloh; instead he would get a priest of his own and worship at home. Before long he not only had a priest, but he convinced other members of the tribe to leave the tabernacle and come to his house, to his priest who was now acting as a fortune-teller. As Micah became more entrenched in his disobedience, he set up idols and a whole new religious order. His actions resulted not only in his death but that of his family, the priest, and all who followed them.

The church is God's idea. Jesus supported the synagogue of his day even while vigorously disagreeing with the religious leaders. We are not excused from going to the place God has designated for worship because some members are not perfect. We are strengthened when we assemble together with others of like faith. There is accountability to others and concerns for those around us as our hearts join together in prayer. 🌸

Day 67

DO I REALLY HAVE TO GO TO CHURCH?

"Let us not give up meeting together, as some are in the habit of doing, but let us encourage one another."
—Hebrews 10:25

PRAYER:
Dear Jesus, I know I often allow myself to be distracted in my worship because of what I think of others. Remind me that though my faults may be different, I am imperfect too. Help me to extend the same mercy and forgiveness to others that you give to me each day. Amen.

Day 68

"But you are a chosen people, a royal priesthood, a holy nation, a people belonging to God, that you may declare the praises of him who called you out of darkness into his wonderful light."
—1 Peter 2:9

I am always amazed at the range of emotional responses to the question, "What would an employer say about you?" Even so, nothing quite prepared me for Mari-Ann. Nervously she clasped and unclasped her hands as she shifted uncomfortably in the chair.

"What would your former boss say about you?" I asked the top of her bent head. For a long minute, nothing but silence, then she softly began to cry. She gave no answer; I could only guess at the extent of her pain as her uneven breathing filled the room.

That interview has stayed with me as a reminder that my life says something to the people around me. What are we saying to the people close to us? My name conjures up a photograph, then an attitude, and maybe some particular habit others have come to associate with my company. The image we present either influences others to want to be followers of Christ or convinces them we have nothing worth keeping after all. Jesus, in his sermon on the mountain said, "Let your light shine before men, that they may see your good deeds and praise your Father in heaven" (Matt. 5:16).

PRAYER:
Lord Jesus, help me to really do as you would do, so others may see your life through me. Amen.

In this story of the man who fell victim to muggers on his way to Jericho, Jesus made one thing perfectly clear: Even if we are prominent members of our society or congregation, we are not pleasing to him until we learn to minister to the despised among us.

How simple it is to tell others what they should do. In fact, both the priest and the Levite were leaders accustomed to establishing rules for others. Yet, faced with a man cruelly beaten, stripped of his clothing and his dignity, the priest and the Levite crossed the road to avoid dealing with him. Their racial prejudices overcame their devotion to God and obliterated the essence of compassion from their lives.

God will not judge us based on who we say we are or on the trappings of our high office. His only concern is that the world, regardless of race, color, or creed, will experience his love and care through us. Then, and only then, will they know we are his disciples.

Day 69

PRACTICING WHAT WE PREACH

Jesus told him,
"Go and do likewise."
—Luke 10:37

PRAYER:
Lord Jesus, I want
to be your hand
extended today to
someone who is
hurting and who
needs the comfort
of your love.
I do not want to be
blind to the oppressed,
deaf to the cry of the
abandoned, or too
busy to stop and be a
friend to the forsaken.
Let me respond as
you would so they will
know you care.
Amen.

Day 70

ALL FOR LOVE

*"If you love me,
you will obey what
I command."*
—John 14:15

Jesus tells the story of two sons in Matthew 21:28–31. The gist of the story is that a farmer had two sons. He asked one to work in the fields, and the son flatly refused but later changed his mind and went. The father then asked the other son if he would join his brother in the field. The second son, without hesitation, said "Yes," but never went. Jesus asked the crowd which of the young men did what his father wanted. Of course, the people agreed that the one who went to the field was the obedient son.

All through his teachings, Jesus made it plain that what we say is not half as important as what we do. It's not enough just to give verbal assent that Jesus is the Son of God. Neither is it proper to know what the Bible says about everything and neglect to practice its teachings in our daily lives. Our actions are the true test of our love for God and our obedience to him.

Like the first son who was called, we may not always feel inclined to obey or see the importance of moving in the moment we are called. However, love of the Father will prevail over our own will and cause us to extend ourselves to please him. ❧

PRAYER:
*Dear father,
let my service be a
reflection of the love
I have for you.
Amen.*

What happens when people attempt to live the Christian life without knowing Jesus? They remain sinners with a thin veneer of holiness on top. Jesus had some unbelievably strong words for some of the so-called religious people of his day. He said that on the outside they appeared righteous to others, but on the inside they were filled with hypocrisy and wickedness. In fact, he called them whitewashed tombs: Clean on the outside, filled with dead men's bones and everything unclean on the inside (Matt. 23:27). Jesus actually said that to people? Oh, yes he did. Jesus knew it was better to offend their sensibilities than to allow them to think that going through the motions was enough to save them from hell.

Coming to Christ means having a change of heart—being sorry for our sins and turning away from them. As we follow Christ, our old desires die, our outlook changes, and we gain a whole new set of priorities. Pleasing God and sharing his love replaces the yearnings to do only what makes us happy or popular with the crowd. Not only do we have new desires, God gives us the Holy Spirit to teach us how to live our new life. He helps us to understand the Bible and brings back the Word to our memory when we need it most. In other words, we are transformed or changed from the inside out. As this occurs, we begin to live like new people, and others soon see the difference Jesus makes. 🌾

Day 71

TRANSFORMED

"Therefore, if anyone is in Christ,
he is a new creation;
the old has gone,
the new has come!"
—2 Corinthians 5:17

PRAYER:
Lord Jesus, I thank you for making me a new person, no longer controlled by sinful habits. Let my life be a witness to others so they may come to know you too.
Amen.

Day 72

LOAN OF A LIFETIME

"You are not your own; you were bought at a price. Therefore honor God with your body."
—1 Corinthians 6:19, 20

When one uses something borrowed, no matter how comfortable the relationship with the lender, the thought is always present that the borrowed item must be returned. This knowledge dictates the manner in which the article is used and the care it receives.

Well, how about our bodies, lives, gifts, and talents? Scripture says these are not our own but are on loan to us from God the Father. Are we living as if we are aware the owner could at any time demand the return of what we glibly call ours? Are we careful about how we use our resources and on whom we shower our most precious treasures? As owner, God ultimately decides what usage is right or wrong. He has the final say.

Jesus' goal is to present us to the Father completely blameless. We become spotless when we live as if bodies are the temples of the Lord. The glory of God abides in us, not behind thick curtains or behind manmade walls. Let's examine again the Lender's conditions and make sure our lives are owner-directed and not borrower-controlled. ❦

PRAYER:
Creator of all things, thank you for the loan of life entrusted to me. I ask for wisdom to use each moment to its fullest, to your glory.
Amen.

Christians today are tempted to temporize, modify, or outright compromise beliefs in order to appear less intolerant and to fit in with the crowd. Before we capitulate and go along to get along, let's see what Christ has to say about the treatment we can expect when we declare ourselves his followers.

"If the world hates you, keep in mind that it hated me first. If you belonged to the world, it would love you as its own. As it is, you do not belong to the world, but I have chosen you out of the world. They will treat you this way because of my name. They hated me without reason" (John 15:18, 19, 21, 25).

The call to follow Christ is not an invitation to popularity and human approbation. Rather, the closer we move to the nature of Christ, the more the world considers us odd, backwards, and unfit for society. Christians are not called to fit in, but are chosen as the salt of the earth and the light of the world. We are Christ's representatives here on earth. His plan is that when others see us, they would instantly be reminded of him. By the same token, we should not be surprised if the world reacts to us in the same manner as they would to him.

Are you hated, belittled, or laughed at? Are you tolerated among your peers only because they have agreed you are weird but harmless? Rejoice and let your heart overflow with songs of triumph at being counted worthy to bear shame for the sake of Christ.

Day 73

Not Popular, but Chosen

"For he chose us in him before the creation of the world to be holy and blameless in his sight."

—Ephesians 1:4

Prayer:

Father, I choose the love of your Son Jesus above fame or popularity. I choose to live in Christ, and to walk with and be like Christ. Amen.

Day 74

NESTING DOLLS

"And your life is now hidden with Christ in God."
—Colossians 3:3

I have always loved Russian Matryoshka dolls. You know, the ones that start with an average-sized doll, which you can open to reveal a smaller one inside, and so on until you reach the smallest one of all, sometimes measuring less than an inch. Today's Bible verse brings to mind a nesting doll set: God, the Father, Jesus, the Son, the Holy Spirit, and me—like the miniature doll, hidden all the way inside. That's a tremendous amount of protection for one human being to have. On a personal level, it means nothing comes to me haphazardly and nothing touches my life without the foreknowledge of the Godhead.

Can this get better? Yes, it can and does. When I feel threatened by circumstances, all I need to do is remember that the Father of creation has no crises. Nothing takes him by surprise. Therefore, he sees ahead of time what my needs will be, and provision is already made. The fact that I am uniquely protected, however, does not deter the plans of the enemy. I am often conscious of storms outside my door. No problem. Jesus says that those who come to him shall never perish, and absolutely nothing can remove them from His hand. Like the smallest Matryoshka, I rest safe in the bosom of the Father.

PRAYER:
My Divine Protector, I am thankful you are so much more than the God of the universe or just some great mystical force. You are my father and I am your child forever protected in the safety of your arms.
Amen.

Though we may derive immense emotional satisfaction from our chosen vocations, we would doubtless admit we also look forward to being paid. Without a doubt, much of the satisfaction we feel would evaporate and we would soon look for new employment if our bosses decided they were no longer able to pay for our services.

As we live from day to day, we also can expect some form of payment for the lives we lived here on earth. Our sinful natures, inherited from Adam, cause us to do things contrary to God's laws. If we live all our lives according to our own agenda, at the end we reap death or separation from God. Of course, we could always try to be holy and hope for the best; the trouble is that God only accepts perfection.

Into that dilemma came Jesus and decided to be our substitute. In other words, he took the payment for all the sins humanity accumulated over the ages and gave us a free, undeserved gift in its place. Justice was outraged and demanded we bear the full measure of our punishment, but God's mercy stilled Justice's strident cries. Today, all we have to do is believe that Jesus took the wage for our sins and receive his gift of eternal life by placing our faith in him. ❦

Day 75

THE WAGE
OR THE GIFT?

"For the wages of sin is death, but the gift of God is eternal life in Christ Jesus our Lord."
—Romans 6:23

PRAYER:
*Dear Lord Jesus,
I believe you loved the world so much you gave yourself so we will not die in our sins but have everlasting life with you.
I accept your sacrifice on my behalf and thank you for your awesome gift.
Amen.*

Day 76

BOUGHT WITH
A PRICE

*"The kingdom of
heaven is like treasure
hidden in a field.
When a man found
it, he hid it again,
and then in his joy
went and sold all he
had and bought
that field."*

—Matthew 13:44

We often refer to our salvation experience as finding a treasure more precious than gold. While this is true, this parable goes beyond our own personal experience. We cannot understand the value God places on us. In spite of our imperfections, he calls us his own peculiar treasure. We are the ones who were buried in the field of sin, our beauty and worth concealed from all but the Creator. Jesus is the one who gave up everything to "buy" us and take us to himself.

The devil convinces many people that they are worthless and, as a result, keeps them subjugated in sinful lifestyles. Long after we come to know Christ and accept his forgiveness, the enemy still tries to condemn us with our past. Child of God, you are infinitely precious in your father's eyes. Your past failures were erased the moment you trusted Christ as Savior. If you do not know him, he died for you because of his great love for you.

You are heaven's treasure.

PRAYER:
*Dear Jesus, you give
my life value and
meaning. You know
all about me and still
call me your jewel.
I thank you for your
unconditional love.
Amen.*

We sing the old Negro spiritual "He's Got the Whole World in His Hands" and give a kind of general assent that God knows everything. On the other hand, it is hard to translate that concept to personal faith and affirm this like Hagar, "You are the God who sees me" (Gen. 16:13).

We see ourselves as too small, too weak, or too sinful to merit God's personal attention. The concept Christ taught his disciples of the importance of lilies, grass, and even sparrows becomes entirely lost on us (Matt. 6:26–30). Loneliness and dead-end situations may challenge our faith, causing us to think that, before God, we are just another face in a sea of faces.

Nothing could be further from the truth. God knows our name. In fact, he tells us that our identity is engraved upon the palms of his hand (Isa. 49:16). You are not a statistic or a cosmic dot floating haphazardly through the mists of time. God knows who you are and daily makes provision for your good. ❧

Day 77

KNOWN OF GOD

And the LORD said to Moses "I know you by name."
—Exodus 33:17

PRAYER:
Dear Jesus, thank you for creating me as I am and for reminding me today that I am precious to you. Help me to see you at work in every area of my life.
Amen.

Day 78

PARALLEL PATHS,
DIFFERENT
DESTINATIONS

*"But small is the gate
and narrow the road
that leads to life, and
only a few find it."*
—Matthew 7:14

H ave you ever driven down a highway and suddenly come upon what I call a double exit—two exits within yards of each other? It always amazes me that though the roads are in such close proximity, they often lead to entirely different parts of town. The informed driver doesn't arbitrarily choose an exit. Rather, one's choice is made relative to the desired destination.

As we travel through life, we encounter paths that at first glance appear to be heading in the direction we want to go. Some are a straight shot, while others, after numerous detours, lead to the desired end. A guide or a directional signal makes all the difference in our choice, whether on the interstate highway or the road of life.

Believers in Christ are blessed with both a guide and a map. Jesus has volunteered to be our guide until death, and the Bible charts the way we should travel. By paying close attention to our map and guide, we avoid being deceived by similarities in directions. Besides, we have the added safeguard of the voice of God whispering behind us, "This is the way; walk in it." ❦

PRAYER:
*Jesus, today I listen
for your still, small
voice as I go about the
business of living.
I will read your Word
and be obedient to
your instructions
for the journey.
Amen.*

A feeling of disbelief and outrage settles on us when we believe we are unfairly treated. The feeling only intensifies if we suspect the insult was intentional. Anger soon follows. Before long, we find ourselves contemplating how to even the score. We brood and imagine "they will say this" and "I will say that," and the umbrage builds.

As Christians, the last thing we need to do is nurture anger. Our imperfect sense of justice can only wreak havoc as we try to resolve every conflict in our favor. Furthermore, if we were allowed to do as our passions dictate, valuable opportunities for God to stretch us would be lost. We would continue in our self-will, and the gentle art of forgiveness would never be learned. I don't have to fly off the handle, yell, or make a scene in order to sin. Seething anger, as an immediate response to problems or conflict, may produce an even more deadly result.

These days the world encourages us to stand up for ourselves, show our strength, and not be pushed around. Conversely, the Bible teaches the quiet strength of self-control. "Better a patient man than a warrior, a man who controls his temper than one who takes a city" (Prov. 16:32). ✿

Day 79

BE SLOW TO GET ANGRY

"Do not be quickly provoked in your spirit, for anger resides in the lap of fools."
—Ecclesiastes 7:9

PRAYER:
Gentle Father, slow me down today. I want to be quick to listen and slow to speak. Help me not to respond in anger to those who offend me, but to demonstrate your peace and forgiveness. Amen.

Day 80

*"These people honor
me with their lips,
but their hearts are
far from me.
They worship me
in vain."*
—Matthew 15:8

The dictionary defines "habit" as an act repeated so often it becomes automatic. Though all habits are not dangerous, many are simply of no value.

Jesus explained to the religious rulers why their worship was meaningless. True, they went to the synagogue daily and dutifully repeated the words they were taught from childhood. The words, however, had no impact on their hearts or lives. What looked like intense devotion to onlookers was nothing more than a mechanical exercise.

It's not enough to go to church and say all the right words and make all the correct responses. More than the formality of rituals, God desires a personal relationship with each of his children. Samson would be the first to testify of going through the motions and having all the right moves without the Spirit of God being present (Judg. 16:20). Rituals will always be a point of affirmation as we worship together, but honoring God from our hearts makes what we do with our hands, lips, and knees effective. ❧

PRAYER:
*Dear Jesus,
I do not want to serve
you just for show.
Let my words and my
actions testify to my
relationship with you.
Amen.*

Five-year-old Tony looked down at his hands for a long time. His aunt had just given him a crisp, new five-dollar bill. Finally, Tony carefully folded it and tore it in two. "This half is for me, and this one is for God," he said.

Do we wonder why Jesus says our attitude should be like a child's? Tony didn't wait and give only when he couldn't stand the urging of conscience anymore. He didn't look for anything in return. He did not worry about whether or not half a bill was enough to take care of his needs. Tony's only concern was making sure he gave to God the portion that belonged to him.

God does not routinely ask for half of what we have. Rather, he asks that whatever he leads us to give, that we give with joy. ✺

Day 81

GOD'S HALF

"Remember this: Whoever sows sparingly will also reap sparingly, and whoever sows generously will also reap generously for God loves a cheerful giver."
—2 Corinthians 9:6, 7

PRAYER:
Father, we thank you for providing for our daily needs. Please accept the gifts we give back to you. Amen.

Day 82

THE WILL OF GOD

*"Therefore do not
be foolish, but
understand what the
Lord's will is."*
—Ephesians 5:17

Being uncertain of God's desire to grant our requests, sometimes causes us to present the same request over and over again in the hope that God will eventually listen. Did God fail to answer, or did we fail to recognize his will for us? When we speak of the will of God, we are agreeing with and voluntarily submitting to God's intent for our lives. We are saying we have discarded our personal agendas and that we are now ready to conform to his program. Should we be surprised when the answer looks nothing like we imagine or even understand? Remember, God does not think like we do. His thoughts are much higher and deeper than ours.

To further compound our schedule, we pray to a God who lives in a different time zone—where a day is a thousand years and a thousand years is a day. In spite of the differences between us and an infinite God we can ask at least three questions to determine whether or not we are praying according to His will.

- Am I in right standing with God? (John 15:7)
- Are the motives behind my prayer pleasing to God? (James 4:2, 3)
- Will I be content if God's answer goes contrary to my expectations? (Matt. 6:10)

PRAYER:
*Dear Lord Jesus,
I know you see far
beyond what I can
understand. Help me
not to rush foolishly
ahead, but to trust
your perfect will.
Amen.*

I gnoring the arm offered to assist her, Kate clutched her pocketbook, gripped the railing, and marched up the steps. She walked into the room and planted herself in the center of the largest sofa. Gold bangles jangled as she adjusted her glasses, then turned to glare at the people in the room. Within moments, what started as a happy family gathering became suffused with tension as her sarcastic words found unfortunate targets. Although life had given her much, her dull, unsmiling eyes, furrowed brow, and turned-down mouth testified to the bitterness and anger raging inside.

Christians are called to share from the abundant treasure of our hearts. This means we should be full of the same words Christ would speak—that is, words of love, faith, peace, joy, and comfort. Christ encountered all types of people in his ministry, even those who were considered to be great sinners. Yet his words never condemned, or belittled any individual. He knew just what to say to build up and to point others to the Father who loved them.

Words that destroy others are not God's idea. Attitudes that rob others of dignity do not glorify the One who calls us not servants, but friends. Being quick tempered may cause us to blurt out things we later wish could be retracted. If that is the case, God can help us to exercise self-control if we submit to his Word and yield our wills to him. ❦

Day 83

WORDS OF GRACE

"Do not let any unwholesome talk come out of your mouths, but only what is helpful for building others up according to their needs, that it may benefit those who listen."
—Ephesians 4:29

PRAYER:
Father, help me today to speak words that build self-esteem in others. Help me not to devalue anyone by my attitude, but to be gracious, portraying your love and grace to others.
In Christ's name.
Amen.

Day 84

LIVING IN REAL TIME

"If anyone is ashamed of me and my words, the Son of Man will be ashamed of him when he comes in his glory and in the glory of the Father and of the holy angels."
—Luke 9:26

The little girl sat hopefully eyeing the wait staff as they passed her table; maybe her turn to be served would come soon. Several minutes elapsed, and still no food. She looked at the hot buttered rolls in the basket and sighed. They sure looked good, but what she really wanted was her dinner. Very quietly, she started to hum. For a moment she forgot the crowded restaurant and even food as her humming blossomed into song.

> Yes, Jesus loves me
> Yes, Jesus loves me
> Yes, Jesus loves me
> The Bible tells me so.

How different is Christianity that is lived from Christianity that is practiced only in certain places, at certain times, on certain days of the week! When the life of Christ becomes our life, we model his image wherever we are. If that child had taken a moment to consider, she might have thought twice about singing "Yes, Jesus loves me" in a crowded restaurant. Why, what would the mommies and daddies think? Instead, she lived what she learned in real time, in the everyday world of hurrying waitresses, burning grease, and tired families gratefully eating meals they did not have to prepare.

Christianity counts most in the humdrum world, surrounded by mundane things, where choir robes and lofty sanctuaries do not compete for our attention to the Word. No wonder we hear it said that the road to heaven bears the footprints of a child.

PRAYER:
Precious Lord, show me how to live as your disciple without shame or hesitation, wherever I am. Amen.

Jesus, in his Sermon on the Mount, instructed his hearers that, if they went to the temple to present their gifts and remembered someone was mad at them, to leave their gifts and correct the situation before approaching the altar again. Such advice is all well and good, but what do you do when your efforts at reconciliation are ignored? Do you go back and retrieve your gift from the altar and promise God to come back again later?

When others withhold forgiveness, it leaves a terrible burden. It really does not matter who is at fault; guilt, anger, and profound sadness often overshadow the lives of the parties involved. The consciousness of being in disfavor with a brother or sister can hinder our communion with the Father. While we should not flippantly disregard the attitude of the person from whom we sought forgiveness, we should be careful we do not become bound by their anger.

Remember Jesus says we are to ask for forgiveness, make a genuine effort to make things right. He did not offer any guarantees that if our repentance was from the heart, we would immediately be forgiven and all would be right with the world. In fact, even after forgiveness is extended, time may still be required before the relationship is completely restored. If it becomes obvious that divine intervention would be needed in order to receive the forgiveness we seek, don't push. Instead, allow the Holy Spirit to reveal other ways to reach out to this person in love. When you are clear in your heart that you have done all you can, walk away and let God deal with the situation in his time. ❧

Day 85

WHEN OTHERS DON'T FORGIVE

"Consider [Jesus] who endured such opposition from sinful men, so that you will not grow weary and lose heart."
—Hebrews 12:3

PRAYER:
Dear Jesus, I forgive those who hurt me and accept your forgiveness for my life. Give me the grace to reach out to them in love, and I trust you to restore fellowship again. Amen.

Day 86

INSTRUCTIONS
FOR A LIFETIME

*"Now we ask you,
brothers, to respect
those who work hard
among you, who are
over you in the
Lord and who
admonish you.
Hold them in the
highest regard in love
because of their work.
Live in peace with
each other. And we
urge you, brothers,
warn those who are
idle, encourage the
timid, help the weak,
be patient with
everyone. Make sure
that nobody pays back
wrong for wrong, but
always try to be kind
to each other and to
everyone else.*

Inspired by the Holy Spirit, Paul closed his letter with enough instructions for us to make it to heaven if the rest of the Bible was taken away.

1. *Respect your leader.* Sometimes we forget that the persons whom God places in leadership suffer the brunt of the enemy's attacks. We seldom remember that they, as wholly dedicated servants, spend numerous hours in prayer and meditation in order to hear from God on our behalf. When believers are disrespectful and callous in their treatment of spiritual leaders, it makes the task of shepherding more difficult. Believers can, through their behavior, hinder their own blessings.

2. *Live in peace with each other.* Like with all families, some members in the body of Christ just rub us the wrong way. This is perfectly natural as we all have different personalities. When Christians accept each other's differences, the devil loses his opportunity to cause small difficulties to escalate into malice, strife, and ultimately hatred.

3. *Warn the idle.* When there seems to be nothing exciting enough in the kingdom of God to employ our energies or we become self-appointed critics of those who are working, Satan has indeed found work for idle hands to do. Christ told the people of his day that the harvest was ripe but laborers were few. The call to active service to win the lost is more urgent today than it has ever been.

4. *Help the weak, be patient with everyone.* Life changes in a moment. Today all might be well with us, and tomorrow our world may lie in shambles at our feet. We might find ourselves needing someone to pick us up and help us carry on. God is pleased when we help those who are weaker than we are. It doesn't matter if it seems like we are covering the same ground over and over again.

(continued next page)

5. *Do not pay back wrong for wrong.* Christ says the world will know that we are his followers when we love one another. True love does not plot revenge; rather it forgives and seeks the good of others even in the face of continued hostility.

6. *Be joyful always.* Does this mean I must always have a smile and nothing will ever go wrong in my life? Don't we all wish such would be the case! Christians, however, can have a core of joy that remains untouched by adversities. This is far removed from happiness—which is dependent on happenings. Our wellspring of joy flows from our assurance of salvation and a personal and permanent relationship with Jesus Christ.

7. *Pray continually.* Impossible, you say? Not if God expects us to do it! We pray continually when we actively seek the presence of God in everything we do. The posture of our hearts captures God's attention, rather than whether we are stopping in traffic so we can kneel.

8. *Give thanks in all circumstances.* Giving thanks seems harder than the previous instruction. When love dies, when financial collapse looms on the horizon, when people wrongfully accuse us, we're supposed to give thanks? Yes. We praise not for what has happened, but for the certainty that our Father never abandons us. We continue to believe he will somehow work everything for our good.

9. *Do not put out the Spirit's fire.* One can kill a blaze by withdrawing fuel, by pouring water, or by smothering the flame with earth. The fire of the Holy Spirit in us, is fueled by the Word, by prayer and fellowship with other believers. When we neglect to add "wood" to fire, the "earth" from a powerless life soon accumulates and smothers what Christ would do in us.

(continued next page)

Day 87

*Be joyful always;
pray continually;
give thanks in all
circumstances, for this
is God's will for you
in Christ Jesus.
Do not put out the
Spirit's fire; do not
treat prophecies
with contempt."*

—1 Thessalonians 5:12–20

PRAYER:
*Father, today I ask
you to open my heart
to honor those who
honor you, to walk in
the way of peace and
to be kind to those
around me for
your sake.
Amen.*

Day 88

10. *Do not treat prophecies with contempt.* People sometimes make the mistake of being so distracted by the messenger that they totally miss the message. Others decide the word is for someone else or that God doesn't speak to individuals today as he did in Bible days. The truth is that God never changes and through the seemingly outdated method of preaching, often by men and women of humble demeanor, God proclaims His Word. We are wise when we listen to preachers of God's Word.

11. *Test everything.* Some have been led in error because of blindly accepting everything everyone says as gospel. The Scripture teaches us to test everything. We do this by looking at the context of the comment, the circumstance under which it was first spoken, and to whom. Next, we compare Scripture with Scripture. In the final analysis, all we believe should be in perfect harmony with the rest of the Scripture as a body; the Bible never contradicts itself.

12. *Hold on to the good.* Be selective. The world offers a plethora of ideologies and philosophies. Christianity insists there can only be one way to everlasting life: through Christ.

13. *Avoid every kind of evil.* The devil is adept at disguising himself as an angel of light in order to trap the unwary. Remember the old adage, "It's better to be safe than sorry." If a course of action looks wrong or feels wrong, take a minute to check before continuing. It probably is wrong.

In concluding the letter (1 Thess. 5:23), the Apostle prays,

> *God keep our souls and bodies blameless until the coming of our Lord and Savior Jesus Christ. Amen.*

Here's a simple exercise: Try putting a spoonful of food in your mouth while your mouth is full of water. Can't do it, can you? Do you know our approach to God can sometimes be the same way? We try to receive new blessings into lives already full with other things.

"Stuff" comes in different guises. It can be worry, busyness, sickness—or anything that makes us preoccupied and diverts our attention from serving God. Before there can be receiving, there has to be an emptying on our part. God wants us to:

- Put away the strange gods or the things so close and dominant in our lives that they block our vision of who he is.
- Be clean through the washing of water (or baptism) and the Word of God, the Bible.
- Change our garments—mind-set, lifestyle, viewpoint, and general direction.
- Then, go up to Bethel, the house of God, symbolizing worship.

We are told, "Blessed are those who hunger and thirst for righteousness, for they will be filled" (Matt. 5:6). God longs to fill our lives with good things, but we must be willing to make room. 🌿

Day 89

GET RID OF THE STUFF

"Get rid of the foreign gods and purify yourselves and change your clothes. Then come and let us go up to Bethel."
—Genesis 35:2, 3

PRAYER:
*Dear Jesus,
I empty myself
of everything that
would crowd out
your presence.
I ask you to come into
my heart today.
Amen.*

Day 90

BE RIGHTEOUS, BELIEVE GOD

Abram believed the
LORD, and he
credited it to him
as righteousness.
—Genesis 15:6

We love to keep balance sheets. We add up all the good deeds, subtract those we should have done, and try to come out on the positive side. In fact, not only do we end up in the black, we can usually find someone who didn't do quite as well as we did.

Jesus told a story of the Pharisee who trusted in his good works and came up really short and the Publican who appealed to the mercies of God and was saved (Luke 18: 10–14). We cannot claim to be righteous based on good works alone. Neither are we required to perform some outstanding feat in order to qualify for salvation. Heaven cannot be earned. God simply asks that we believe in the Lord Jesus Christ and accept his righteousness. ❦

PRAYER:
Lord Jesus, I know
I cannot make it to
heaven except by your
righteousness. I trust
in you and not the
works of my hands.
Amen.

Catalysts are agents that provoke or speed up significant change or action. In the body of Christ, the church, we are all agents for change. Some are magnificently gifted and are sent to the upper echelons of society, while others are called to minister to the poor and the outcasts of the world. Even Christ's genealogy proves the kingdom consists of all classes of humanity.

The Bible displays one example after another of God accomplishing his will through widows and orphans, kings and peasants, the aged and the youth, through the erudite and through simple fishermen. This happens because we, the believers, are not the main ingredients. Rather, we are receptacles of the glorious treasure of the Holy Spirit, to the glory of God. We may be small and think in the eyes of the world that we are mere grasshoppers, yet the Father uses us with amazing effectiveness when we are small in our own eyes and allow him to bring change through us. Are we willing to forgo being the main thing and just be a catalyst for kingdom occurrences? ✲

Day 91

PRAYER:
Father, sometimes I'm uncomfortable just working in the background. I think of places I have been and what I have done in the past, and I keenly feel the lack of recognition I now encounter every day. Help me to be willing to accept that you have placed me at this place where I can be of the most good to your kingdom. I want to serve you faithfully. Amen.

Day 92

*"The LORD
said to Moses,
"Make a snake and
put it up on a pole;
anyone who is
bitten can look at it
and live."*

—Numbers 21:8

PRAYER:
*Dear Lord Jesus,
thank you for taking
the curse of the cross
and making it an
everlasting blessing.
Thank you for your
power to also take the
ugly and despised
things of my life and
transform them into
objects for your glory.
Amen.*

God pronounced a curse upon the serpent the day it conned Eve into sinning. The serpent lost its inherent grace and beauty and became instead the symbol of treachery and evil. God used snakes to punish the Israelites when they sinned in complaining against him as they traveled through the wilderness. Many died from the poisonous bites, and those who lived suffered unspeakable agony as the venom attacked their systems.

Why, then, would God use such an unlikely totem as a symbol of healing? When the multitude repented, God told Moses to make a serpent of bronze and place it on a pole. All those who looked at that snake would be healed.

The people could hardly know this was but the first act in a drama to be continued hundreds of years later. The disciples were doubtless familiar with the law that places a curse on everyone who hangs on a tree (Gal. 3:13). Jesus foretold His own death by saying, "Just as Moses lifted up the snake in the desert, so the Son of Man must be lifted up, that everyone who believes in Him may have eternal life" (John 3:14, 15).

Like the snake, the cross symbolizes a death so painful and a curse so complete the condemned was executed outside the city limits. This is the mystery of salvation: that two of the most repulsive tokens in human history, both representative of death and suffering, brought us salvation and eternal life.

Modern cynicism teaches that everyone and everything has its price. If we believe that, then we also accept there is nothing or no one we cannot corrupt with money.

But what if we are already sold? "Bought with a price—not silver, gold, or perishable stuff, but with the blood of Christ (1 Pet. 1:18)? It is a liberating experience when we say by our actions that we are not for sale and we will not be enticed away from our obedience to Christ.

Pressure to conform or "sell out" can come from any angle as we search for fulfillment and recognition in our careers and daily pursuits. It is infinitely easier to fudge a little on some issues, to give silent agreement to others, and to just "go with the flow" in general, than to be the lone voice of dissent. Still, being sold out to God means he can count on us to stand our ground even when challenged by people in authority. What will our testing be? Maybe the powers-that-be have already hinted that in order to be considered for a promotion you should lighten up a little and try harder to fit in. Remember Balaam's answer. God's children are not for sale. ❧

Day 93

ALREADY SOLD

But Balaam answered them, "Even if Balak gave me his palace filled with silver and gold, I could not do anything great or small to go beyond the command of the LORD my God."
—Numbers 22:18

PRAYER:
Father, please give your children everywhere a steadfast determination to please you and to be true to you, whatever the cost. Amen.

Day 94

ALL FOR LOVE

*If you love me,
you will obey
what I command.*
—John 14:15

I n Matthew 21:28–31 Jesus tells the story of two sons. The gist of the story is that a farmer had two sons. He asked one to go work in the fields, and the son flatly refused but later changed his mind and went. The father then asked the other if he would join his brother in the field, and this son, without hesitation, said yes, but never went. Jesus asked the crowd which of the boys did what his father wanted. Of course the people agreed that the one who went to the field was the obedient son.

Over and over again as Jesus taught, he emphasized the fact that what we say is not half as important as what we do. It is not enough just to give verbal assent that Jesus is the Son of God and that He died for our sins. Neither is it okay to know what the Bible says about everything and neglect to practice its teachings in our daily lives. Our actions are the true test of our love for God and our obedience to Him.

Like the first son who was called, we may not always feel inclined to obey or see the importance of moving the moment we are called. However, love for our Father will prevail over our own desires, and we will find ourselves doing all that we can to please Him. ❧

PRAYER:
*Dear Lord Jesus,
let my life be a
reflection of the love
that I have for you.
Amen.*

Have you ever considered the privilege we have in Christ, to be able to come before him at any time? A relationship without the blood sacrifices and mediating priest was something Old Testament saints couldn't even imagine, yet it all became possible for us when Jesus died.

We read that when he said from the cross, "It is finished," the veil separating the common people from the Holy of Holies tore from the top down, giving free access to all. Simultaneously, he took away the laws and commandments that condemned us at every step, covered us with his own righteousness, and forever pledged himself to be our advocate with the Father. After Jesus completed his earthly mission, he sent the Holy Spirit to be a friend, teacher, helper, and guide to us who are now the inheritors of salvation.

How close, then, does that make him? Closer than breath, because it is "in him we live and move and have our being" (Acts 17:28). We no longer have to make arduous pilgrimages to find God, because we are his dwelling place; he lives in us (2 Cor. 6:16). How near is he? Just as close as a whispered prayer, and he promises he will never go away. 🌿

Day 95

How Close Is He?

"What other nation is so great as to have their gods near them the way the LORD our God is near us whenever we pray to him?"
—Deuteronomy 4:7

PRAYER:
God of the universe, you have chosen my heart as your temple. Thank you for opening up the way to your presence by the blood of Jesus Christ. Amen.

Day 96

ENTERING INTO WORSHIP

"And they were calling to one another: "Holy, holy, holy is the LORD Almighty; the whole earth is full of his glory."
—Isaiah 6:3

The glory of God or the manifest presence of God always follows true worship. One can only imagine what Isaiah felt as he heard the echo of the seraphs as they extolled the holiness of God. The power of their praise was such that it shook the doorpost and the foyer of the temple, and the entire building was filled with smoke. Solomon had a similar experience at the dedication of the temple. After 120 priests blew their trumpets and all the singers joined in praise and worship, the glory of the Lord so filled the house that the priests were unable to go in and perform their duties (2 Chr. 5:11–14).

The twenty-first-century church, for the most part, has yet to see a true manifestation of God's glory. This may be because words of praise are hurriedly tacked on to the end of prayers, or they are used as introductions to our wish lists. Unencumbered praise desires nothing of God but himself, and it finds complete fulfillment in knowing God is glorified. ✤

PRAYER:
Almighty Father, I lay aside my requests for blessings and praise you for who you are. You are God, and you alone are worthy of worship and praise. Amen.

The Lord's Prayer represents one of the best known pieces of literature today. It is so much a part of our common experience the words are often repeated without conscious thought of their meaning. Nevertheless, an important principle lies behind the phrase "forgive us as we forgive those who trespass against us." In this passage we see reciprocity at work. Jesus himself made it plain when he said that if we do not forgive others when they do us wrong, neither will our heavenly Father forgive us when we sin (Matt. 6:12, 14, 15).

Sincerity when we pray will not move the heart of God if we have unsettled issues with others. Rather, we are admonished to confess our faults and make sure we have trusted Christ's sacrifice for our forgiveness. The answer to our prayers and the peace of a close relationship with God are open to us as we graciously dispense with ill feelings toward those who cause us distress. 🌿

Day 97

HINDRANCES TO WORSHIP

"If I had cherished sin in my heart, the Lord would not have listened"
—Psalm 66:18

PRAYER:
Dear Lord Jesus, I present

[insert a name or names]
to you. I willingly forgive and release (them, him, her) into your care. I affirm, from this moment on, I will no longer carry this burden of anger and bitterness, and I accept your forgiveness for my sins. Amen.

Day 98

REFLECTED GLORY

*"[Moses] was not
aware that his face
was radiant because
he had spoken with
the LORD."*
—Exodus 34:29

Moses did what no one had done before. He saw God face-to-face. After his prolonged exposure to the glory of God, a change came over him. His body, though mortal and completely unlike that of God, began to absorb radiance; Moses glowed. His face was so bright when he finally left the mountaintop, the people were afraid to get close to him.

Being in the presence of God brings change. Time spent in prayer and listening to his voice through the Bible fills the soul with such light that others can't help but know we have "seen" God. Our faces may not shine as Moses' did, but our character will. Peace, joy, gentleness, and patience will radiate from us. Our praise will be exuberant and tireless as our very natures are changed and we begin to reflect the glory of God in our daily lives.

PRAYER:
*Dear Jesus,
I rejoice in the glory
of your presence as
I spend time with you
each day. Let my life
reflect the graces
found in you.
Amen.*

Jesus decided to visit the home of Mary, Martha, and Lazarus. Martha bustled about making sure the house was clean, the linen was aired, and that fresh water was in the jars. She made a hundred trips to the kitchen and worried whether there would be enough food for Jesus and his friends. Finally, worn out with all her nervous rushing about, she came to Jesus, asking him to tell her sister Mary to help with the preparations. Jesus answered "You are worried and upset about many things, but only one thing is needed. Mary has chosen what is better, and it will not be taken away from her" (Luke 10:41, 42). All Martha did was necessary, but her timing and focus were wrong. She never gave herself a chance to hear what Jesus had to say.

We must have a means of livelihood, a way to care for those entrusted to us. Still, we should never be so concerned about today's physical needs that we neglect to set aside time to tend to our spirit. Material things and the satisfaction of having a well-ordered household are powerless to bring us closer to God. Our spiritual man can only be awakened and nurtured by the Word of God. Jesus asked, "What good is it for a man to gain the whole world, yet forfeit his soul? Or what can a man give in exchange for his soul?" (Mark 8:36, 37).

Day 99

SETTING PRIORITIES

Man does not live on bread alone but on every word that comes from the mouth of the LORD.
—Deuteronomy 8:3

PRAYER:
Lord, sometimes it's hard to set priorities when I'm pressured to give immediate attention to so many things. Help me to put you first. Then please bring order to the rest of my life. Amen.

Day 100

SALVATION TO OVERFLOW

"But now it was a river that I could not cross, because the water had risen and was deep enough to swim in."

—Ezekiel 47:5

When repentance initially touches one's heart, the individual is brought out of sin; their feet, as it were, are removed from slippery places and firmly planted upon a rock. This rock represents Christ and the salvation he offers. Now the choice remains: Move from the salvation experience into deeper life with God, or remain content with just being saved.

The river that Ezekiel saw issuing from under the throne became progressively deeper the farther he went. God, like the man with the measure, wants to take us to deeper places in him. As we mature in our Christian relationship, we should be deeper in faith, love, mercy, and all the virtues Christ demonstrates. In time, God moves from the distant realm of "somewhere out there" to being a close, personal friend.

As the reality of this union hits home, we are pulled away from the relative safety of basic Christian principles into the deeper waters of true discipleship and daily commitment to Christ. Inevitably we grow until we eventually plunge with complete abandon into the marvelous ocean of God's grace. We learn to swim, buoyed by the power of the Holy Spirit.

What complete wonder breaks upon our souls when we first meet Jesus and get our feet wet with the thought of being saved from sin! Yet, dear child of God, nothing compares with the glory of total surrender as he becomes, for us, water deep enough to swim in. ❧

PRAYER:
*My Father,
move me beyond the
tameness of head
knowledge into the
deep waters of being
totally yielded to you.
Amen.*

God loves to do makeovers. He takes the ugly and seemingly valueless things, and the people that the world casts aside as hopeless, and gives them a place of honor. Manoah was resigned to the fact that he had no son to bear his name. If he were a rich man, he could procure a steward and, in time, make him his heir. A steward, however, was far beyond anything Manoah could afford.

His wife carried her guilt in silence, always hoping and praying, year after year, that she would have a son. She watched as her body changed and hope slowly diminished, then faded all together as her season of life passed. When childbearing was impossible, the angel came with the promise of a son. The fulfillment of that promise made all the difference in the world.

It does not matter if we think our youth is spent—God has power beyond anything we can imagine. If you are faced with a barren, hopeless situation today, remember that God says, "Behold, I make all things new." Give the problem to Jesus and rejoice in the knowledge that he takes hopeless situations, broken spirits, and destroyed lives and creates a source of blessing for generations to come. 🌿

Day 101

BEFORE AND AFTER

"You are sterile and childless, but you are going to conceive and have a son."
—Judges 13:3

PRAYER:
Father, I confess there are many seemingly broken and barren things in my life that I am unable to change. Make them over into sources of blessing, I pray in Jesus' name. Amen.

Day 102

THE GIFT OF TODAY

Now listen, you who say, "Today or tomorrow we will go to this or that city, spend a year there, carry on business and make money." Why, you do not even know what will happen tomorrow.

—James 4:13, 14

Mr. Jay lived in a cramped one-room trailer, alone except for a big shaggy black dog named Blue and two tiny black kittens. The trailer sat at the farthest end of the park, at the edge of the lake in a run-down fishing village. A morose and taciturn man, Mr. Jay seldom spoke during the hour it took to perform the numerous tasks associated with his care. One day as I discussed with him his plan of care for the next six weeks, Mr. Jay abruptly began to speak. Feelings long repressed charged to the surface. His eyes filled with tears, and he began his life story.

Both he and his wife had a dream of leaving the cold, icy winters of the north and retiring to a place where the sun shone year round. To that end, they skipped vacations, lived as frugally as they could, and were just barely able to purchase a home in a trailer park and a small fishing boat. A year or two into their dream, Mrs. Jay died after a brief illness. Heartbroken, Mr. Jay stayed on at the village trying to deal with his loss the best way he could. An unfortunate incident with a rust nail caused him to be taken to the hospital, and because he could not remember the last time he had a checkup, the doctor did a thorough physical as well. Blood tests revealed a blood sugar level way over 400, and all other tests indicated advanced diabetes. Mr. Jay blinked back the tears as he looked at the stump that used to be his heel.

"Everything fell apart, Nurse," he said. "If you can do something with your husband or your children, don't wait," he continued. "We planned for so many years, and my wife and I only had one year of retirement together.

(continued next page)

Four years ago when I stepped on that nail, I did not know. Now every few months I have another surgery. My doctor and I both know it's only a matter of time before the whole leg goes. Live, Nurse. Live today," he ended and lapsed into silence.

Mr. Jay's retirement was a far cry from what he anticipated. Still, the despair of his final years served as a sobering reminder of the value of time and the fact that living, once postponed, cannot be rescheduled. 🌸

Day 102

Day 103

THE MAN WHO WOULDN'T BE KING

But Gideon told them, "I will not rule over you, nor will my son rule over you."
—Judges 8:23

Gideon's humility never allowed him to take himself or his abilities seriously. He did not become engorged with pride when the angel called him a mighty warrior (Judg. 6:12). Nor did he gain an exaggerated sense of greatness when, with three hundred soldiers, he defeated the Midianite army. Israel, on the other hand, wanted to do something for their benefactor. They decided to make Gideon king. He would have had the honor of being Israel's first king and the founder of its first dynasty. Gideon was not tempted. He recognized God's theocratic government and reminded the people that God was their king, and he alone should rule over them.

Being gifted in special ways or having God use us to bring blessing to the body of Christ in one way or another does not mean that he wants us to be "leaders" from this point on. There is no title required to be a dedicated disciple. We need only be obedient and willing to let God be king. ✻

PRAYER:
Dear Jesus, today I ask you to show me ways that I can serve others and bring honor to your name. Amen.

Every blessing of God comes with a condition attached: if you do this, then I will do that. In our eagerness, we often rush to the end of the promises and pay scant attention to what is required of us. Most of what God has pledged himself to do for us requires that we:

- carefully listen to him
- do what is pleasing to him
- obey his commandments
- keep his laws

The terms are very clear and leave little room for misinterpretation. The key to the desires of our hearts is in our hands. We go first by demonstrating a willingness to obey what God says. Then we can be sure he will do all he has promised to do. 🌿

Day 104

YOU GO FIRST

He said, "If you listen carefully to the voice of the LORD your God and do what is right in his eyes, if you pay attention to his commands and keep all his decrees, I will not bring on you any of the diseases I brought on the Egyptians."
—Exodus 15:26

PRAYER:
Dear Jesus, I rely on your strength to help me keep my part of the bargain and be obedient to you. Thank you for the blessings you have promised. Amen.

Day 105

HOME SCHOOLING

"Fix these words of mine in your hearts and minds. Teach them to your children, talking about them when you sit at home and when you walk along the road, when you lie down and when you get up."

—Deuteronomy 11:18, 19

PRAYER:
Divine Teacher, show me creative ways to communicate your words to this new generation. Let me be a living example of what a believer should be. Amen.

Every day, technology pushes us to do things faster. As the pressures increase, we fall back on the time we should be spending with our families to complete the tasks we could not quite finish at the office. Or we work late, allowing ourselves only enough time to grab a bite to eat and fall into bed, in order to start the whole sequence again tomorrow. This mad rush through life is even harder on the single parent, who has to be everywhere and play multiple roles. Some parents simply rely too heavily on "child development centers" to teach their children about Jesus. Others squeeze in a lesson here and there and hope for the best.

Unfortunately, that is not quite the plan God had in mind. He wants us to teach our children at home by lifestyle. Christianity lived in the everyday world is easily communicated. It only becomes confusing and ineffective when our actions differ from what we profess. For example, by praying with our children and inviting them to pray during trying situations, we are teaching them the value of prayer. When we give thanks for our food at the table and openly express thanks to God for meeting our needs, our children learn thankfulness. In the same way, setting aside time to take them to church for worship shows them that praising God is not just something for the elderly or the unpopular, but for everyone. Parents have the most influence on children. Let us live what we believe and use every opportunity to teach our children how to be men and women of faith.

The story of Balak and the prophet Balaam, whom Balak hired to put a curse on Israel, is told in Numbers 22–24. Balak soon discovered his hatred of Israel could not change God's blessings into a curse. Balaam finally told this evil king, "God has blessed [Israel], and I cannot change it" (Num. 23:20).

The devil may hate us, throw everything he has at us, but as believers in Christ we are blessed. If, like Job, we find ourselves stripped of all our possessions and our health, or if those near and dear to us tragically disappear from our lives, we are still blessed. Our future is still secure in God.

The world hates us because we are not a part of its system. Our refusal to partner with or entertain sinful actions sometimes causes us to be labeled intolerant, bigoted, or out of touch with the real world. Jesus, on the other hand, says that we are blessed because we do not walk in the council of the wicked but we delight in the law of the Lord. Christians represent a different kingdom, one that is destined to completely overthrow the devil.

Do the world and the devil hate you? Jesus says, "Rejoice, for great is your reward in heaven" (Matt. 5:11, 12). ✾

Day 106

HATED BUT BLESSED

"Esau held a grudge against Jacob because of the blessing his father had given him."
—Genesis 27:41

PRAYER:
Dear Jesus, you told us that though we are blessed, we would be hated and despised because we follow you. Help us not to be discouraged but to joyfully point others to you.
Amen.

Day 107

GREAT BLESSINGS, GREAT PRICE

"After you have suffered a little while, [God] will himself restore you and make you strong, firm and steadfast."
—1 Peter 5:10

PRAYER:
Dear Lord, I will not complain about the things in my life that cause me difficulty. Instead, I will see them as stepping-stones to greater blessings. Amen.

Most of us desire the good things of life: prosperity and the rewards of affluence. Needless to say, we seldom think about what it would actually cost to have our fondest wishes fulfilled.

David, as the youngest son, lived the life of a shepherd. His most exciting occurrence was battling wild animals that would prey on the sheep. Then God anointed him to be the next king. David had no chance to be taught his new job. Instead he learned how to be a good soldier and a good general running from cave to cave, trying to stay one step ahead of Saul and his assassins.

Many times as we study the Bible we revel in the beauty of the psalms and joy in the majesty of the throne of David. We forget these are but the end results of severe adversity. The great apostle Paul started out as an enemy of the church and doubtless carried the sting of all he did to hinder the work of Christ to the end of his days. He spent much of his life in prison for the gospel. But from those precious years came the letters to the churches to serve as roadmaps for believers then, now, and for countless generations to come. Christ, our greatest example, came to earth and was hated and rejected by those who should have cherished him the most. Yet he persevered, hating the agony of the cross but ever looking forward to the blessing of redemption for all humanity. Now he sits at the right hand of the Father, forever victorious.

Are you paying a high price for the blessing you desire? Rejoice—your triumph is just ahead. ❧

Where exactly was Joseph when this statement was made of him? He was just sold by his brothers as a slave to a bunch of Ishmaelite traders. Yet, when Potiphar, the captain of Pharaoh's guard, looked at Joseph, he saw a young man destined for greatness. This youth went up through the ranks from being an Israelite slave to becoming Potiphar's steward. One could not have guessed that being thrown in prison was actually a step forward. Joseph went from a lowly prisoner to second ruler over the land of Egypt.

Our present situation is not necessarily an indication of where we are destined to be. God uses all kinds of methods and some rather strange tools to hone the bravest soldiers in his kingdom. Take heart and serve well wherever God places you. If the dungeon becomes a part of your journey, like Paul and Silas, sing praises until deliverance occurs (Acts 16:25, 26). When those you have helped forget you, humble yourself under the mighty hand of him who will lift you up in his own time (1 Pet. 5:6). God is the one who ultimately decides your future, and as an heir and equal partner with Christ, you are already destined for the throne.

Day 108

PROSPEROUS WHILE
DISPOSSESSED

*The LORD was
with Joseph and . . .
the LORD gave
him success in
everything he did.*
—Genesis 39:2, 3

PRAYER:
*Lord Jesus, I know
my future is secure in
you. Thank you, for
making everything
work for my good.
Amen.*

Day 109

*"Now the Spirit of the
LORD had departed
from Saul."*
—1 Samuel 16:14

How did Saul, someone who started out with such great promise, end up losing his connection with God? Maybe because he never quite understood that God's plan and purpose for his life (and the nation of Israel) required walking in absolute *trust*. Shortly after he was crowned king, Saul's son Jonathan attacked a Philistine outpost. The Philistines retaliated by assembling a massive army against Israel. King Saul moved his army to Gilgal to await the arrival of the prophet Samuel to sacrifice on Israel's behalf.

When Israel's army saw the size of the enemy's forces and realized an entire week had passed without any sign of Samuel, they began to scatter. King Saul panicked, took matters into his own hands, and offered the sacrifice. He was not even a member of the priestly tribe. His actions marked the beginning of a long journey into madness and his eventual death by his own hands on the battlefield.

God's ways are not our ways, nor do we understand, until after the fact, why he insists on doing things his way. However, true happiness and his continued favor are only promised when we walk in his will. We do well to remember the words of Samuel to the rejected king: "To obey is better than sacrifice, and to heed is better than the fat of rams" (1 Sam. 15:22). ✣

PRAYER:
*Heavenly Father,
I humbly ask you
to forgive my
stubbornness and the
times when my self-
will led me away from
what was pleasing to
you. Help me to wait
on you even when
there seems to be no
visible answer.
Amen.*

One of the biggest obstacles in our walk with God is our terrible memory. When things are horrible we are penitent and give the greatest attention to reading our Bibles and spending time in prayer. We do all we can to get God's attention. When life gets good again, we say a brief thank-you-Lord and slip into complacency. We may not refer to our jobs or personal affairs as gods. Yet our lives often become cluttered with people and things to the exclusion of adequate time for prayer and meditation.

As we read through the Old Testament, we see these words: "and Israel sinned" or "and they did evil in the sight of the Lord," over and over again. God would raise up a nation to punish them, Israel would repent, only to continue the cycle as soon as the judgment passed. Finally, God told them there would come a day when he just would not save them anymore.

The best time to demonstrate our love for God and our interest in what he has to say to us is when there is no pressure. Once we have established this relationship, we never have to worry whether he will be with us or not when things are tough, nor will we entertain thoughts of deserting to the enemy's camp. Rainy-day conversions may help in a pinch, but only a lifetime relationship brings the assurance of salvation. ❧

Day 110

RAINY-DAY REVIVAL

"But you have forsaken me and served other gods, so I will no longer save you. Go and cry to the gods you have chosen. Let them save you when you are in trouble."
—Judges 10:13, 14

PRAYER:
*Jesus, I accept you as my Lord and Savior in good times and when I am pressured by adversity.
I choose to walk with you always.
Amen.*

Day 111

BEYOND WHERE YOU ARE

"The LORD said to Abram after Lot had parted from him, "Lift up your eyes from where you are."
—Genesis 13:14

The preceding chapters in Genesis tell of the call of Abram. God told him to remove himself from his family and nation and go to a place that God would show him. Abraham obeyed and started the journey by faith, with no idea what the final destination would be. Lot, on the other hand, had no sense of destiny and didn't understand Abraham's call. He just followed.

As the head of the family, Abraham had first choice of water, grazing, and campsite. Yet, he graciously surrendered his right to Lot, who immediately chose all the best spots. Before Abraham could regret his decision to give Lot first preference, God spoke to him. Abraham had a revelation of the full scope of what being a father of nations would entail. God told him the blessing would extend beyond where his eyes could see or his feet could touch, to countless generations to come.

If Abraham had held on to his rights, he may have missed the benefits God intended for him. Are we allowing something or someone close to us to block our view of God's greater plan for us? The possibilities are truly endless when we get glimpses of life beyond where we are.

PRAYER:
Father, help me to look beyond the obstacles and to remain focused on your divine plan and purpose for me. Amen.

Jacob's obvious favoritism drove a wedge between his children that nothing but the grace of God could remove. Jacob always had Joseph's best interests in mind. If one looks back to the fateful meeting between Jacob and his brother Esau, even as death threatened, Jacob still remembered to place Joseph and his mother at the very back of the caravan. His reasoning was that if things really became ugly, then Joseph would be far enough from the confrontation to have time to escape.

I have heard some people say that Jacob had to do what he did in order for God to fulfill his plan. Hardly. God does not need us to do the wrong thing for the right reasons. He is well able to bring about his purpose independent of our actions. All our children deserve an equal place in our hearts. One child should never be elevated while the other is discounted. The way we communicate with each child may be different, but there should never be any doubt in their minds they are loved and that they are indescribably dear to us.

Jesus gives us an example of inclusive love by placing words like "whosoever," "all," and "as many" throughout the Bible. He doesn't single out any of us to favor above the other; instead he calls us all "friends" and he addresses believers as "joint heirs" of the heavenly kingdom. Today, you are one of his dear children, and his only desire is that you accept his amazing love. 🌿

Day 112

LOVES ME, LOVES ME NOT

"Now Israel loved Joseph more than any of his other sons. When his brothers saw that they hated him and could not speak a kind word to [Joseph]."
—Genesis 37:34

PRAYER:
*Dear Father, thank you for making me your child and for giving me complete acceptance as your child.
Amen.*

115

Day 113

Who Is Writing the Rules?

"And even Judah did not keep the commands of the LORD their God. They followed the practices Israel had introduced."
—2 Kings 17:19

People seldom have a problem keeping rules. Most of us would just prefer to make and follow our own. What happens when we espouse our own practices over what God has outlined for us? Well, we lose the blessings that follow obedience. For example, honoring parents brings long life, trusting in the Lord assures us of protection and prosperity wherever we live, and giving to the Lord ensures that our storehouses will always have plenty.

It is perfectly reasonable to suppose walking in our own way has its consequences too. Prosperity often comes at a high price when the laws of God are ignored. Israel decided to get away from the restrictions of the law and do their own thing. They probably felt freedom for a while, but before long, they became slaves to the nations around them. Not only were they in physical bondage, they also lost the nearness of God as their comfort. In time, they realized that following God was their best choice after all. Do we want to take the chance of writing our own rules and missing out on our benefits now and in eternity?

PRAYER:
Father, I believe in your greater wisdom in laying down the path I should follow. I resist my own rules and choose instead to follow your way. Amen.

No one could have predicted Joseph's success. We watch his catastrophic descent into slavery and imprisonment, and gasp in amazement at his meteoric rise to grand vizier of Egypt. What was his secret? Maybe Zechariah gives the best answer. "I am the LORD All-Powerful. So don't depend on your own power or strength, but on my Spirit" (Zech. 4:6, CEV). Joseph had the Spirit of the Lord, and the Spirit accomplished in him all God desired. By the Spirit he was able to help his fellow prisoners, be wisdom to Pharaoh, and savior to his people.

David prayed in Psalm 51:11 that God would not take the Holy Spirit from him. He came to grips with the idea that the Spirit of God in us makes us who we are. At times it's hard to forgive those who are cruel to us. We wonder why God allows others to harm us, and if we are not careful, we become cold and bitter. When, however, we tap into the strength God provides, we not only forgive, but the world recognizes us as one in whom the Spirit dwells. 🌾

Day 114

THE SPIRIT MAKES THE DIFFERENCE

"So Pharaoh asked them, "Can we find anyone like this man, one in whom is the Spirit of God?"
—Genesis 41:38

PRAYER:
Dear Jesus, thank you for your Holy Spirit living in me. I draw upon your strength to accomplish your will and to be a witness to those around me.
Amen.

Day 115

EXPOSED

And "[you] may be
sure that your sins
will find you out."
—Numbers 32:23

Very early in the life of the New Testament church, the Holy Spirit taught a graphic lesson about the importance of walking the talk. Ananias and Sapphira were members of the local church and outwardly did everything expected of them. When the practice of communal living was instituted, they seemed to be all for it.

They sold their home and all they had and gave the proceeds to the disciples—or so it appeared. Ananias insisted, when questioned, that the portion he brought to the church was the total amount from the sale. Peter took him to task for lying, not to the disciples, but to the Holy Spirit. At Peter's declaration, Ananias fell dead at his feet. Sapphira came in after a little while, and her story was consistent with the one her husband told. Without hesitancy, she declared that all the money had indeed been given to the disciples. She lived only long enough to know her Ananias was already dead for telling the same lie.

What was their crime? They were dishonest with God. Did they die because they wanted to save something for their old age? No. It was not about money, but all about motive. Ananias and his wife gave to keep up appearances and for the recognition their actions would bring. No matter how much we impress others with our talk, in the long run our walk will prove who we really are. God is looking for people who will forgo the bells and whistles of public acclaim and just be true to him.

PRAYER:
Heavenly Father,
I open all the secret
places of my heart to
you in complete
honesty. Let my life
be a true reflection of
the words I speak.
Amen.

What would happen if the lighthouse keeper allowed the light to go out? Quite possibly, some vessel would run aground in the shallows or be dashed to pieces on the reefs. Christ tells us we are lights, cities positioned on a hill, visible from afar. What happens when our lights go out? Our world, without a sense of direction, suffers shipwreck.

Many conditions threaten the constancy of our light: media, the politics of the day, and laws that speak more authoritatively than our voices, to name a few. It becomes increasingly easy to do what is politically correct and remain silent. Jeremiah came to a place in his life where he contemplated remaining quiescent. "But if I say, 'I will not mention him or speak any more in his name', his word is in my heart like a fire, a fire shut up in my bones. I am weary of holding it in; indeed, I cannot" (Jer. 20:9). Why couldn't the prophet keep silent? Too much was at stake.

The same is true of the fire on the altar of the tabernacle, the fire in the prophet, the flame in the lighthouse, and the fire of our testimony. All these fires must burn continuously because too much stands to be lost if the fires go out. Lives are being lost for the lack of a dependable light. Jesus is counting on us to shine and lead others to him. Your light may not be as big or as strong as you want it to be, but good news: even the tiniest light is a threat to darkness.

Day 116

MAINTAINING THE FIRE

"The fire must be kept burning on the altar continuously; it must not go out."
—Leviticus 6:13

PRAYER:
Father, I seldom feel my voice is important enough to make a difference, and so I serve in silence. Help me not to be distracted by the smallness of my light or the darkness of sin surrounding me. Help me shine—to tell others about your love and forgiveness, in Christ's name. Amen.

Day 117

EVERYTHING IS ALL RIGHT

*"Are you all right?
Is your husband all
right? Is your child all
right?" "Everything is
all right," she said.*
—2 Kings 4:26

Everyone worked at fever pitch, hoping to complete the harvest before the rains started. The small boy bustled along beside his father, faithfully imitating his every move, but somehow managing to be more in the way than being of actual help. His father smiled indulgently at him, reveling in the miracle of the child being there at all. He and his wife had long given up hope of ever having children. Even when the prophet thanked them for their kindness by promising them a child, they saw it as little more than the customary blessing given to a good host. Yet, there he was, this small boy, the spitting image of his mother. The child, as if conscious of his father's thoughts, looked up and smiled at him, and the old man felt his heart contract with the force of the love he felt.

One moment, the child smiled; the next, he was screaming, "My head, my head," before crumpling and falling awkwardly against his father's leg. Forgetting the harvest at least momentarily, the servant gently picked up the child. "He has only fainted master," he said trying to speak reassuringly. Let me take him back to the house, his mother will know what to do."

The servant prayed as he galloped across the broken field, cradling the slight figure of the child in the crook of his arm. Breathlessly, he dismounted once he approached the prophet's quarters from the main courtyard. "Let my lord Elisha be there," the servant prayed. Only silence echoed his anguish as he turned to leave the empty bedchamber. Now he had no choice but to tell his master's wife that her son was dead.

"Lay the child on the prophet's bed," she said from behind him.

"My lady, shall I call the mourners?" the servant asked.

(continued next page)

"No, call no one. Tell no one. My son will be all right."

Silently, the servant closed the door and followed the woman. He wished she would cry or scream, anything, but this terrible silence. Her pace quickened as she neared the harvest field.

"Husband!" she cried as she came within earshot. "I have need of a donkey and a servant."

"Why? Where are you going?" he asked.

She forced her tone to sound casual as she replied, "To bring the prophet home."

"Why go today?" he husband asked. "It's not the New Moon or the Sabbath."

"It's all right to fetch him," she replied.

Out of sight of her husband and the reapers, she told the servant to ride as fast as he could. "And do not slow down unless I tell you to," she added. Clinging tightly to the reigns she hardly felt the jarring as the little donkey sped over the uneven ground. Her mind went back to the excitement of being a bride and the anticipation of bearing a son. She remembered the moments of anticipation that turned to anxiety, and the feelings of anxiety that morphed into resignation as the years hurried by while she remained childless. Her husband never reproached her or complained, but she knew he grieved at having no heir. Then, Elisha entered their lives. First a meal, then a few nights lodging whenever he was in the area, until finally they built him a room of his own. She smiled in spite of herself as she remembered her overwhelming joy as she discovered she was with child—just like the prophet promised.

"He will not die!" she shouted into the wind. "He will be all right."

Elisha listened as the sounds of hoof-beats came closer, sensing the urgency, even though

(continued next page)

Day 117

Day 117

the riders were still some distance away. He stared into the roiling dust, straining to recognize the figures approaching with such haste. "No, it can't be," he muttered, "but it is. That is the Shunammite. But what is she doing here, this time of day? Why would she come? Here, Gehazi, go meet her and ask her if everything is all right," Elisha said.

In a short while Gehazi returned with the report. "My lord Elisha, she will not speak until she stands before you. She said, 'Tell your master, everything is all right.'"

Fear and panic gave rise to anger as the Shunammite faced the prophet. "Did I ask you for a son, my lord? Didn't I tell you, don't raise my hopes?" she demanded.

The child, thought Elisha. *Was something was wrong with the child? Was everything truly all right?* The prophet mounted his donkey, and the small party started down the mountain trail. Finally, dusty and tired, they reached the village. Elisha raced up the stairs to the tiny bedroom where the child was and softly closed the door behind him. The old prophet drew an uneven breath, willing the tightness in his chest to subside. He looked at the small boy on the bed with dirt smudges like brown ink splashes against now colorless cheeks.

This would not be easy, death would be loathe to release its innocent captive. He silently breathed a prayer to the Giver of all Life and felt the energy of the Spirit thrilling through his being with an intensity he had never felt before. Instinctively, he knew that he had only moments to cover the child with his body, to breathe life back into him.

To the woman and the servant waiting below, it seemed like eons passed before the prophet finally reappeared, bringing the boy

(continued next page)

122

with him. Tears held in check until now, cascaded in a joyous flood as the mother embraced her son. Everything was at last all right.

Sometimes we have difficulty accepting that even the dreadful things in our lives are needed if God's will is to be accomplished. Like this mother so long ago, we can refuse to doubt and take our troubles back to the one who gave us the gift of life and the assurance of his presence. We can choose to believe that, in spite of the evidence of our eyes, everything is all right. 🌺

Day 117

PRAYER:
Father, you tell us in everything we should give thanks because everything works for the good of those who love you and are called to your purpose. By faith, we know all is well. Amen.

Day 118

NOT GOOD ENOUGH

"Remember the words I spoke to you: 'no servant is greater than his master.'"
—John 15:20

I drove as fast as I dared and prayed that I would make it to the patient on time. His sister sounded so frantic on the phone that there was no way to guess what kind of disaster awaited me. Mr. Kurtz did not live in my case management area, but as the nurse on call over the weekend, the emergency visits fell to me.

Old Willow-Pond Road had very few lights, and the street signs were either down or so poorly painted that they were unreadable in the darkness. Fortunately, there were not many houses after the intersection, so it was fairly simple to figure out where the Kurtzes lived. Miss Kurtz met me at the gate, flashlight in hand. The naked twenty-watt bulb suspended on thin black electric wires on the porch did little to discourage the blackness of the walkway. She took my nursing bag while I grabbed one of almost everything from the supplies in my car trunk.

Miss Kurtz had been talking since I pulled up at the gate. "Nurse, I'm so sorry you had to come out at this awful hour and with the street so dark an' all. I couldn't do anything with him tonight. Everything I did was wrong, and he went off into one of his rages and started pulling things."

"Before I knew it, there was blood everywhere and I just didn't know what to do. I'm sorry, maybe I should have just waited until morning," she finished almost inaudibly.

We were at her brother's door before I had a chance to do more than give her a reassuring smile. "Hello, Mr. Kurtz," I said, pausing briefly on the threshold. "GET OUT! What are you comin' in for?" he exclaimed violently.

(continued next page)

Mary's eyes filled with tears as she handed me my bag. "I'll be in the kitchen if you need me," she whispered.

Suddenly, Mr. Kurtz looked up as if noticing me for the first time. His face turned bright red and registered acute disgust as he drawled, "You're all they could find?"

Miss Kurtz, who hadn't quite made it to the kitchen, was wringing her hands. "Billy Joe, please, please calm down and let the nurse help you," she begged.

The room looked like a cyclone had passed through. Sheets were wadded up and lying all over the floor, the heparin lock port dangled uselessly from Billy Joe's arm, but the fluids were nowhere to be seen. The urine catheter hung over the bed rail, spreading an ever widening circle on the floor. I looked at the bloodstained bed and the trailing, unconnected intravenous lines and figured an hour-and-a-half visit—if I was lucky.

"Yep, Mr. Kurtz, I'm all you are getting tonight," I replied with a rueful smile. The minutes ticked by with Mr. Kurtz cursing minorities on the one hand while his sister apologized and begged him to be quiet from the doorway. Methodically I went from one task to the next. First a bath, then clean sheets, relocate new IV fluids—on and on through the bitter tirade. *What made this old broken-down man better than me?* I fumed silently. *How dare he call me those filthy names? I did not have to help him, even if I was on call. I could call the office and ask them to send the relief nurse. Why should I have to put up with this horrible verbal abuse?* Outwardly calm and reassuring for Miss Kurtz's sake, inside I burned with anger and resentment.

"Remember Jesus," something inside me whispered. *How I hate being in this house,* I raged

(continued next page)

Day 118

silently. *"Remember Jesus,"* the words came again. *What do you mean remember Jesus? What does that have to do with anything?* I questioned.

Softly, the voice began to remind me of Jesus' rejection. He, too, came to help because only he could deliver man from sin. Instead of the world embracing him, they scorned him, called him a sinner, a drunkard, and every vile name they could think of. Jesus never responded in kind or sought to justify his position. Instead, he simply did the work he came to do with the utmost love.

Suddenly, Billy Joe's ranting did not matter anymore. As he struggled to come up with another racial slur, I smiled at him and told him my name again. I employed every bit of my nursing skill to make Billy Joe's care as painless as possible, and gradually his belligerence faded. Remembering Christ and the hostility he suffered gave me strength to give loving care to a frightened, unhappy old man. *

PRAYER:
*Dear Jesus,
sometimes it's not
easy to love those who
insult and mistreat us.
Help me to remember
that the servant is not
greater than the
master. Thank you
for lovingly enduring
shame for my sake.
Amen.*

Have you ever been asked to introduce yourself to a group? Perhaps you were asked to say your name, where you are from, and some personal data in about two minutes. A million thoughts run through your mind. What can you say for a whole two minutes?

Now here's a good story. Moses is having his first face-to-face encounter with God, and God is giving him a message for Pharaoh. Moses accepts the directive, then quite naturally asks, "Suppose I go to the Israelites and they ask me, 'What is [your] name?' Then what shall I tell them?" (Exod. 3:13). In other words, tell me a bit about yourself.

God replies, "I AM."

Moses looks in the direction of the voice and says, "Yes, I'm listening."

God then says, "That's it. I AM has sent you."

Moses scratches his head in puzzlement and begins to explain. "Lord, you don't understand. I have lived at court. I know that when an ambassador visits Pharaoh, the herald goes before and proclaims the glories of the king being represented, the dominions of the kingdom, and the gifts being presented to Pharaoh. I am slow of speech, but—

"Moses, Moses," God quietly interrupts. "I am Alpha and Omega, the Ancient of Days, without beginning and without ending.

"I am complete within myself, self-existing, self-perpetuating, before time, outlasting eternity.

"I sit above the circle of the earth, transcendent, yet intimately involved with my creation.

"I gave the stars their morning song, and the sun is but a diffuse reflection of my glory.

Day 119

I AM

God said to Moses, "I AM who I AM."
—Exodus 3:14

(continued next page)

Day 119

"The unseen heavens declare the marvels of my hand, and the vastness of the universe is but a minute glimpse of my domain.

"The wind is my chariot and my attendants are clothed in fire.

"I AM. And by me everything exists."

By then Moses' bafflement knew no bounds. He looked at his feet and asked, "Lord, is it all right with you if I go back to the first message? I'll just tell them what you said before. You know, 'I Am.' Let's give Pharaoh something he might understand."

"That's what I said," God replied.

The book of Job asks, "Can you fathom the mysteries of God? Can you probe the limits of the Almighty? They are higher than the heavens—what can you do? They are deeper than the depths of the grave—what can you know? Their measure is longer than the earth and wider than the sea" (Job 11:7–9). When one really considers it, "I AM" is truly the most comprehensive answer God could give, the only one that covers all he was, is, and always shall be.

Fifteen East had a sampling of every form of human misery since Adam. It became the perfect floor to orient new graduate nurses brimming with all the knowledge they could not wait to apply.

Richard knew he was playing a losing hand against death, and nothing could shake his terror at the thought of dying. At night, he refused to have his lights turned off. He fought the sleep-inducing effects of his pain medication only to fall into an exhausted slumber with the coming of dawn. As the cancer consumed his body, eating became difficult for him. He seldom tolerated meal supplements, and we could only watch helplessly as he slowly began fading away. Every weekend, I was sure that I was seeing him for the last time, but somehow he held on.

One morning just as I finished his bath and medication, he asked a question. "Nurse, do you think God will forgive me?"

"Of course," I replied. "God forgives anyone who asks him."

"But Nurse, you don't understand," Richard persisted. As I closed the curtains, he quietly told me his story. After he finished, I shared with him God's plan of salvation and invited him to believe Christ died not just for everyone, but for him, personally. He asked Jesus to forgive him and come into his heart, and I continued my rounds. Richard died a few weekends following that encounter. He went to be with the Lord in the morning, with the lights on.

Sooner or later, we will come to the place where we face death, our own or that of someone close to us. In either case, we need not be afraid. Jesus promises a place of everlasting light, joy, and gladness for all those who love him and accept the forgiveness he so freely offers.

Day 120

DON'T TURN OUT THE LIGHTS

There will be no more night. They will not need the light of a lamp or the light of the sun, for the Lord God, will give them light.
—Revelation 22:5

PRAYER:
Lord Jesus, I love you and thank you for forgiving my sins. I look forward to the wonderful home you have prepared for me, to live in the light of your presence forever. Amen.

Dear Reader:

Did you know that keeping a prayer journal will actually improve the quality of your prayer life? Journaling serves to:

- build faith through your own personal encounters with God
- broaden your prayer horizons as you intercede about issues of global significance as well as personal affairs
- provide clear hindsight into God's wisdom in saying "No" or "Wait" to the petitions dearest to your heart

To get started, simply turn the page and enter the date and your prayer request. Then wait in faith for the answer. As your entries multiply, your confidence in God and what the apostle James calls "effective, fervent prayer" will also blossom (James 5:16).

May God bless you as you start your journey of faith.

—*Lauren Erika Myers*